FLASHMAPS
NEW YORK

Editor
Steven K. Amsterdam

Creative Director
Fabrizio La Rocca

Cartographer
David Lindroth

Designer
Tigist Getachew

Editorial Contributors
Robert Blake
Helayne Schiff

Cartographic Contributors
Edward Faherty
Sheila Levin
Page Lindroth
Vicki Robinson
Eric Rudolph

D0818278

Fodor's Travel Publications, Inc.
New York • Toronto • London • Sydney • Auckland
http://www.fodors.com/

Contents

Copyright © 1996 by Fodor's Travel Publications, Inc.

Fodor's is a registered trademark of Fodor's Travel Publications, Inc. Flashmaps is a registered trademark of Newberry Award Records, Inc.

Special Sales

Fodor's Travel Publications are available at special discounts for bulk purchases for sales promotions or premiums. Special editions, including personalized covers, excerpts of existing guides, and corporate imprints, can be created in large quantities for special needs. For more information, contact your local bookseller or write to Special Markets, Fodor's Travel Publications, 201 East 50th St., New York, NY 10022. Inquiries from Canada should be directed to your local Canadian bookseller or sent to Random House of Canada, Ltd., Marketing Dept., 1265 Aerowood Dr., Mississauga, Ontario L4W 1B9. Inquiries from the United Kingdom should be sent to Fodor's Travel Publications, 20 Vauxhall Bridge Rd., London, England SW1V 2SA. **ISBN 0-679-03019-0**

PRINTED IN THE UNITED STATES OF AMERICA 10 9 8 7 6 5 4 3 2 1

Area Codes: Manhattan (212); Bronx, Brooklyn, Queens, Staten Island (718); Nassau & Suffolk (516); Northern NJ (201). All (212) unless otherwise noted.

EMERGENCIES

AAA Emergency Road Service ☎ 800/222-4357

Ambulance, Fire, Police ☎ 911

Animal Bites ☎ 566-2068

Animal Medical Center ☎ 838-8100

Arson Hotline ☎ 718/722-3600

Battered Women ☎ 800/621-4673

Child Abuse ☎ 800/342-3720

Deaf Emergency ☎ 718/899-8800

Dental Emergency ☎ 677-2510

Domestic Violence ☎ 800/621-4673

Drug Abuse ☎ 800/395-3400

Emergency Medical Technician (EMT) Information ☎ 718/416-7000

Missing Persons ☎ 719-9000

Park Emergencies ☎ 800/201-5722

Poison Control ☎ 340-4494

Rape Hotline ☎ 577-7777

Runaway Hotline ☎ 966-8000

Sex Crimes Reports ☎ 267-7273

Suicide Prevention ☎ 532-2400

Victim Services Hotline ☎ 577-7777

SERVICES

AAA ☎ 757-2000

AIDS Hotline ☎ 800/342-2437

Alcoholics Anonymous ☎ 870-3400

All Night Pharmacy ☎ 755-2266

Amex Lost Travelers Checks ☎ 800/221-7282

ASPCA ☎ 876-7700

Better Business Bureau ☎ 533-6200

Borough President ☎ 669-8300

Bridges & Tunnels ☎ 360-3000

Central Park Events ☎ 360-8126

Chamber of Commerce ☎ 493-7400

Chequepoint USA ☎ 869-6281

City Sanitation ☎ 219-8090

Consumer Affairs ☎ 487-4398

Convention & Visitor's Bureau ☎ 397-8222

Customs (24 hr.) ☎ 800/697-3662

Department of Aging ☎ 442-1000

Disabled Information ☎ 229-3000

Foreign Exchange Rates ☎ 883-0400

Foreign Newspapers ☎ 840-1868

Gay and Lesbian Switchboard ☎ 777-1800

Health Department ☎ 442-1999

Health Information (24 hr.) ☎ 434-2000

Housing Authority ☎ 306-3000

Immigration/Naturalization ☎ 206-6500

Legal Aid Society ☎ 577-3300

Mayor's Office ☎ 788-7585

Medicaid ☎ 718/291-1900

Medicare ☎ 800/638-6833

New York Post Office ☎ 967-8585

NY Public Library Information ☎ 661-7220

Passport Information ☎ 399-5290

Planned Parenthood ☎ 541-7800

Potholes ☎ 442-7094

Salvation Army ☎ 337-7200

Sidewalks ☎ 442-7942

Social Security ☎ 800/772-1213

Supreme Court ☎ 374-8500

Taxi Complaints ☎ 302-8294

Telegrams ☎ 800/325-6000

Time ☎ 976-8463

Towaways ☎ 971-0770

Traffic Information ☎ 442-7080

Traveler's Aid ☎ 944-0013

UN Information ☎ 963-1234

US Customs ☎ 466-5550

Weather ☎ 976-2828

24-Hour Locksmith ☎ 247-6747

TOURS

Adventure on a Shoestring ☎ 265-2663

Art Tours ☎ 239-4160

Backstage on Broadway ☎ 575-8065

Circle Line ☎ 563-3200

Doorways to Design ☎ 718/339-1542

Ellis Island Ferry ☎ 269-5755

Gray Line ☎ 397-2600

Harlem Renaissance ☎ 722-9534

Island Helicopter ☎ 564-9290

Manhattan Sightseeing ☎ 354-5122

NY Walks ☎ 797-2388

The Petrel (1938) ☎ 825-1976

The Pioneer (1885) ☎ 669-9417

Seaport Line ☎ 608-9840

Short Line ☎ 736-4700

Sidewalks of NY ☎ 517-0201

Spirit of NY ☎ 727-2789
Statue of Liberty Ferry ☎ 269-5755
TNT Hydrolines ☎ 800/262-8743
World Yacht Cruises ☎ 630-8100

PARKS AND RECREATION
Annual Sporting Events ☎ 465-6000
Acqueduct Race Track
☎ 718/641-4700
Belmont Raceway ☎ 718/641-4700
Brendan Byrne Arena
☎ 201/935-3900
Bryant Park Tickets ☎ 382-2323
Giants Stadium ☎ 201/935-8222
Jets Information ☎ 516/538-7200
Madison Square Garden
☎ 465-6741
Meadowlands Arena
☎ 201/935-3900
Meadowlands Race Track
☎ 201/460-4079
NY Knicks Hot Line ☎ 465-5867
Nassau Coliseum ☎ 516/794-4100
NYC Marathon ☎ 860-4455
Parks Events ☎ 360-1333
Parks & Recreation ☎ 408-0100
Shea Stadium ☎ 718/507-8499
Sports Phone ☎ 976-1313
US Open Tennis ☎ 718/271-5100
Yankee Stadium ☎ 760-6200
Yonkers Raceway ☎ 914/968-4200
Zoo/Central Park ☎ 861-6030
Zoo/Bronx ☎ 718/367-1010

TRANSPORTATION
Adirondack Pine Hill Trailways
☎ 800/225-6815
Amtrak ☎ 582-6875; 800/523-8720
Bonanza Bus Lines ☎ 800/556-3815
Bus & Subway ☎ 718/330-1234
Bus & Subway Access
☎ 718/596-8585
**George Washington Bridge Bus
Station** ☎ 564-1114
Greyhound Bus Lines ☎ 971-6300
Hoboken Ferry (NJ) ☎ 201/420-4422
JFK Airport ☎ 718/244-4444
JFK Bus Transportation
☎ 718/632-0506
JFK Express (train to plane)
☎ 718/858-7272
JFK Parking ☎ 718/656-5699
LaGuardia Airport ☎ 718/476-5000
LaGuardia Bus Transportation
☎ 718/476-5353

LaGuardia Ferry ☎ 800/54-FERRY
LaGuardia Parking ☎ 718/476-5000
Long Island Railroad (LIRR)
☎ 718/217-5477
Manhattan Helicopter ☎ 967-6464
Martz Trailways ☎ 800/233-8604
Metro North ☎ 532-4900
Newark Airport ☎ 201/961-6000
Newark Bus Transportation
☎ 201/762-5100
Newark Parking ☎ 201/623-6334
NJ Transit ☎ 800/626-7433;
201/762-5100
New York Helicopter
☎ 800/645-3494
PATH ☎ 800/234-7284
Passenger Ship Terminal
☎ 246-5451
Peter Pan Bus Lines ☎ 413/781-2900
Port Authority Bridges and Tunnels
☎ 360-3000
Port Authority Bus Terminal
☎ 564-8484
Port Authority Helicopter
☎ 248-7240
Roosevelt Island Tram ☎ 832-4543
Staten Island Ferry ☎ 718/390-5253
Vermont Transit ☎ 802/862-9671

ENTERTAINMENT
Alliance of Resident Theatres
☎ 989-5257
The Big Apple Circus ☎ 268-2500
Carnegie Hall ☎ 247-7800
City Center ☎ 581-7907
HIT-TIX (Music) ☎ 564-8038
Jazz Line ☎ 479-7888
League of American Theatres
☎ 764-1122
Lincoln Center ☎ 875-5000
Movie Phone ☎ 777-FILM
NYC On Stage ☎ 725-1174
Parents League of NY ☎ 737-7385
Radio City Music Hall ☎ 247-4777
**Reduced Price Theatre Tickets
(TKTS)** ☎ 768-1818
Tickets (Bryant Park) ☎ 382-2323
Ticketmaster ☎ 307-7171
Telecharge ☎ 239-6200

MAP 1 **Metropolitan Area**

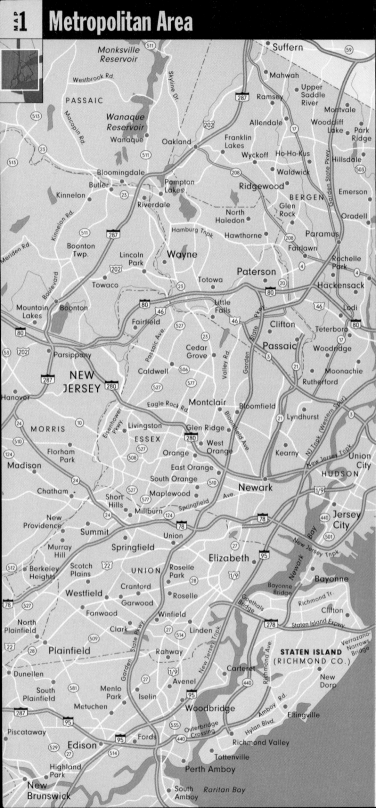

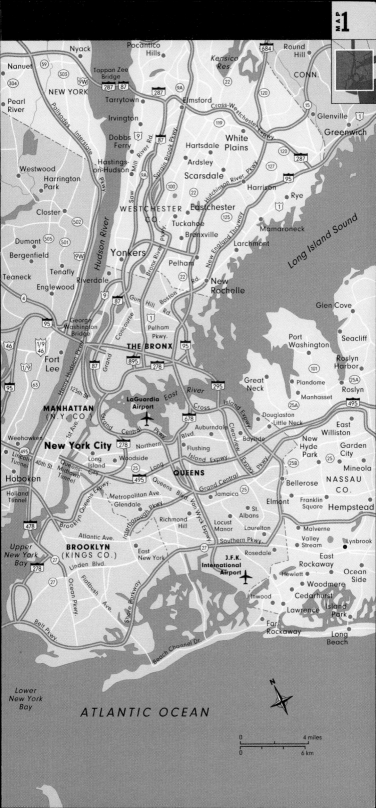

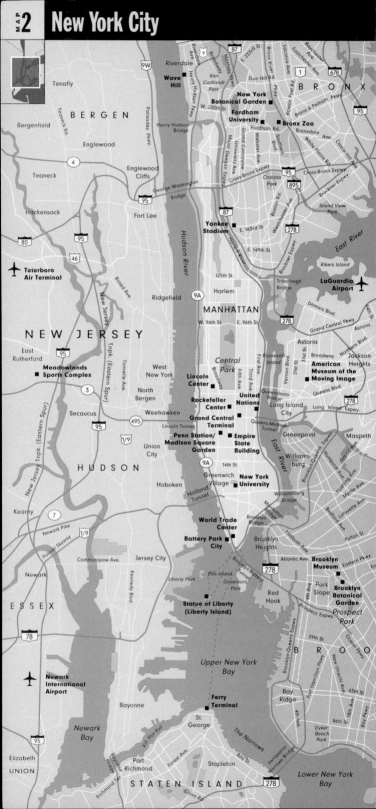

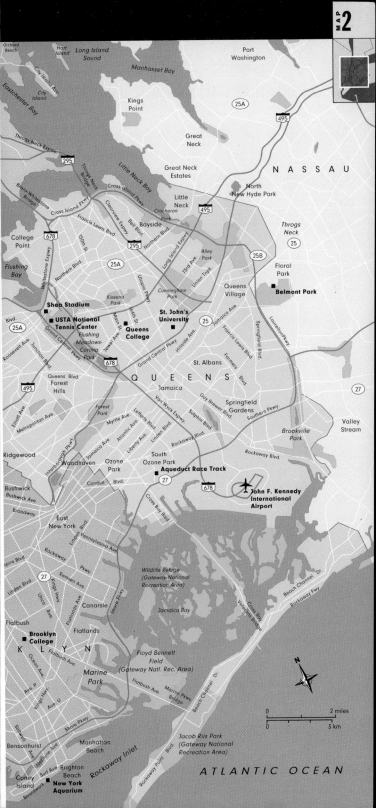

MAP 3 **Manhattan/Uptown**

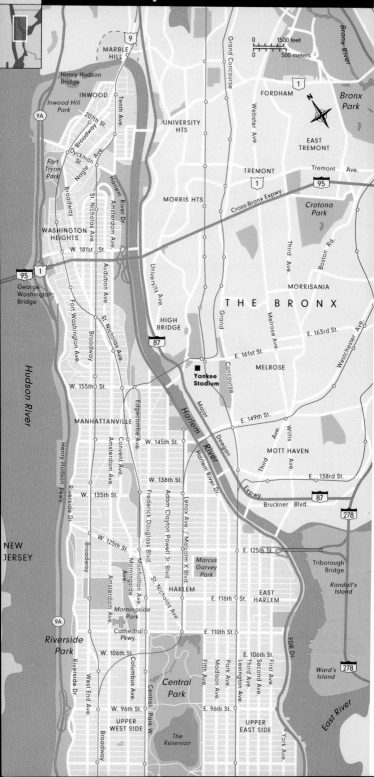

Manhattan/Downtown

MAP 4

MAP 5 — Manhattan Neighborhoods

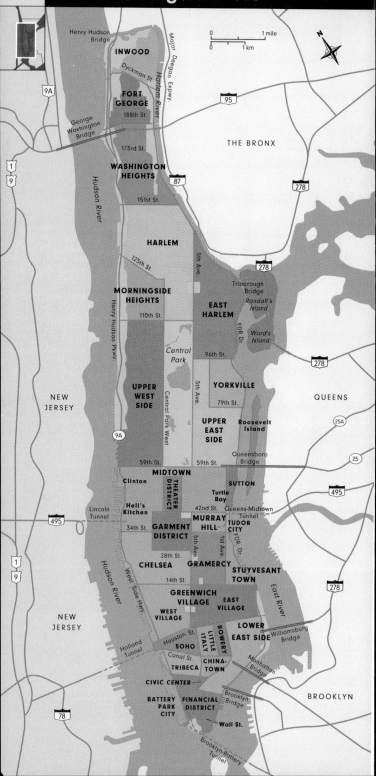

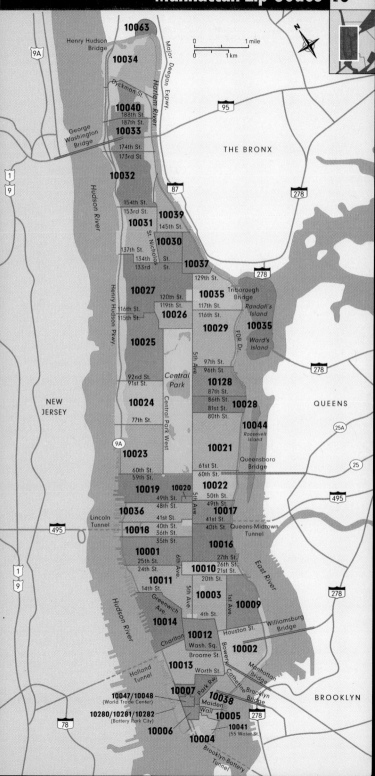

10063

Henry Hudson Bridge

9A

10034

Dyckman St.

Major Deegan Expwy.

Harlem River

10040
188th St.
187th St.

George Washington Bridge

10033
174th St.
173rd St.

1
9

10032

THE BRONX

95

87

278

154th St.
153rd St.

10039
145th St.

St. Nicholas

10031

10030
137th St.
134th St.
133rd St.

10037
129th St.

10027
120th St.
119th St.
116th St.
115th St.

10026

Henry Hudson Pkwy.

Hudson River

10035

Triborough Bridge

117th St.
116th St.

Randall's Island

10029

10035

FDR Dr.

Ward's Island

278

10025

5th Ave.

97th St.
96th St.

Central Park

92nd St.
91st St.

10128

87th St.
86th St.
81st St.
80th St.

10028

NEW JERSEY

10024

77th St.

Central Park West

10044
Roosevelt Island

QUEENS

25A

9A

10023

60th St.
59th St.

10021

61st St.
60th St.

Queensboro Bridge

25

10019

49th St.
48th St.

10020

10022
50th St.
49th St.

5th Ave.

495

10036

Lincoln Tunnel

495

10018
41st St.
40th St.
36th St.
35th St.

10017
41st St.
40th St.

Queens-Midtown Tunnel

10001
25th St.
24th St.

10016

6th Ave.

10011
14th St.

10010
20th St.

27th St.
26th St.
21st St.

East River

278

Greenwich Ave.

5th Ave.

10003

4th St.

1st Ave.

10009

10014

Charlton

10012
Wash. Sq.
Broome St.

Houston St.

Williamsburg Bridge

Hudson River

10013

Holland Tunnel

Worth St.

Bowery

Catherine St.

10002

Manhattan Bridge

Park Row

Brooklyn Bridge

BROOKLYN

10047/10048
(World Trade Center)

10007

10038
Maiden Lane

10280/10281/10282
(Battery Park City)

10005

10006

10041
(55 Water St.)

10004

Brooklyn-Battery Tunnel

78

278

MAP 7 **Avenue Address Finder**

Streets	West End Ave.	Broadway	Amsterdam Ave.	Columbus Ave.	Central Park West		
94-96	700-737	2520-2554	702-733	701-740	350-360		
92-94	660-699	2476-2519	656-701	661-700	322-336		
90-92	620-659	2440-2475	620-655	621-660	300-320		
88-90	578-619	2401-2439	580-619	581-620	279-295		
86-88	540-577	2361-2400	540-579	541-580	262-275		
84-86	500-539	2321-2360	500-539	501-540	241-257		
82-84	460-499	2281-2320	460-499	461-500	212-239		
80-82	420-459	2241-2280	420-459	421-460	211		
78-80	380-419	2201-2240	380-419	381-420	American Museum of Natural History		
76-78	340-379	2161-2200	340-379	341-380			
74-76	300-339	2121-2160	300-339	301-340	145-160		
72-74	262-299	2081-2114	261-299	261-300	121-135		
70-72	221-261	2040-2079	221-260	221-260	101-115		
68-70	176-220	1999-2030	181-220	181-220	80-99		
66-68	122-175	1961-1998	140-180	141-180	65-79		
64-66	74-121	1920-1960	100-139	101-140	50-55		
62-64	44-73	Lincoln Center	60-99	61-100	25-33		
60-62	20-43	1841-1880	20-59	21-60	15		
58-60	2-19	Columbus Circle	1-19	2-20	Columbus Circle		

	11th Ave.	Broadway	10th Ave.	9th Ave.	8th Ave.	7th Ave.	6th Ave.
56-58	823-854	1752-1791	852-889	864-907	946-992	888-921	1381-1419
54-56	775-822	1710-1751	812-851	824-863	908-945	842-887	1341-1377
52-54	741-774	1674-1709	772-811	782-823	870-907	798-841	1301-1330
50-52	701-740	1634-1673	737-770	742-781	830-869	761-797	1261-1297
48-50	665-700	1596-1633	686-735	702-741	791-829	720-760	1221-1260
46-48	625-664	1551-1595	654-685	662-701	735-790	701-719	1180-1217
44-46	589-624	1514-1550	614-653	622-661	701-734	Times Square	1141-1178
42-44	553-588	1472-1513	576-613	582-621	661-700		1100-1140
40-42	503-552	1440-1471	538-575	Port Authority	620-660	560-598	1061-1097
38-40	480-502	1400-1439	502-537		570-619	522-559	1020-1060
36-38	431-471	1352-1399	466-501	468-501	520-569	482-521	981-1019
34-36	405-430	Macy's	430-465	432-467	480-519	442-481	Herald Square
32-34	360-404	1260-1282	380-429	412-431	442-479	Penn Station	
30-32	319-359	1220-1279	341-379	Post Office	403-441	362-399	855-892
28-30	282-318	1178-1219	314-340	314-351	362-402	322-361	815-844
26-28	242-281	1135-1177	288-313	262-313	321-361	282-321	775-814
24-26	202-241	1100-1134	239-287	230-261	281-320	244-281	733-774
22-24	162-201	940-1099	210-238	198-229	236-280	210-243	696-732
20-22	120-161	902-939	162-209	167-197	198-235	170-209	656-695
18-20	82-119	873-901	130-161	128-166	162-197	134-169	613-655
16-18	54-81	21-872	92-129	92-127	126-161	100-133	574-612
14-16	26-53	Union Square	58-91	91-44	80-125	64-99	573-530

Crosstown Street Address Finder

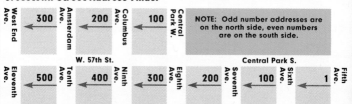

West End Ave. ← 300 Amsterdam Ave. ← 200 Columbus Ave. ← 100 Central Park W.

NOTE: Odd number addresses are on the north side, even numbers are on the south side.

W. 57th St.

Central Park S.

Eleventh Ave. ← 500 Tenth Ave. ← 400 Ninth Ave. ← 300 Eighth Ave. ← 200 Seventh Ave. ← 100 Sixth Ave. ← 1 Fifth Ave.

MAP 7

5th Ave.	Madison Ave.	Park Ave.	Lexington Ave.	3rd Ave.	2nd Ave.	1st Ave.	Streets
1130–1148	1340–1379	1199–1236	1449–1486	1678–1709	1817–1868	1817–1855	**94–96**
1109–1125	1295–1335	1160–1192	1400–1444	1644–1677	1766–1808	1780–1811	**92–94**
1090–1107	1254–1294	1120–1155	1361–1396	1601–1643	1736–1763	1740–1779	**90–92**
1070–1089	1220–1250	1080–1114	1311–1355	1568–1602	1700–1739	1701–1735	**88–90**
1050–1069	1178–1221	1044–1076	1280–1301	1530–1566	1660–1698	1652–1689	**86–88**
1030–1048	1130–1171	1000–1035	1248–1278	1490–1529	1624–1659	1618–1651	**84–86**
1010–1028	1090–1128	960–993	1210–1248	1450–1489	1584–1623	1578–1617	**82–84**
990–1009	1058–1088	916–959	1164–1209	1410–1449	1538–1583	1540–1577	**80–82**
970–989	1012–1046	878–911	1120–1161	1374–1409	1498–1537	1495–1539	**78–80**
950–969	974–1006	840–877	1080–1116	1330–1373	1456–1497	1462–1494	**76–78**
930–947	940–970	799–830	1036–1071	1290–1329	1420–1454	1429–1460	**74–76**
910–929	896–939	760–791	1004–1032	1250–1289	1389–1417	1344–1384	**72–74**
895–907	856–872	720–755	962–993	1210–1249	1328–1363	1306–1343	**70–72**
870–885	813–850	680–715	926–961	1166–1208	1296–1327	1266–1300	**68–70**
850–860	772–811	640–679	900–922	1130–1165	1260–1295	1222–1260	**66–68**
830–849	733–771	600–639	841–886	1084–1129	1222–1259	1168–1221	**64–66**
810–828	690–727	560–599	803–842	1050–1083	1180–1221	1130–1167	**62–64**
790–807	654–680	520–559	770–802	1010–1049	1140–1197	1102–1129	**60–62**
755–789	621–649	476–519	722–759	972–1009	**Queensborough Bridge**		**58–60**
720–754	572–611	434–475	677–721	942–968	1066–1101	1026–1063	**56–58**
680–719	532–568	408–430	636–665	894–933	1028–1062	985–1021	**54–56**
656–679	500–531	360–399	596–629	856–893	984–1027	945–984	**52–54**
626–655	452–488	320–350	556–593	818–855	944–983	889–944	**50–52**
600–625	412–444	280–300	518–555	776–817	902–943	860–888	**48–50**
562–599	377–400	240–277	476–515	741–775	862–891	827	**46–48**
530–561	346–375	Met Life (200)	441–475	702–735	824–860	785 United Nations	**44–46**
500–529	316–345		395–435	660–701	793–823		**42–44**
460–499	284–315	Grand Central	354–394	622–659	746–773	**Tudor City**	**40–42**
424–459	250–283	68–99	314–353	578–621	707–747	666–701	**38–40**
392–423	218–249	40–67	284–311	542–577	666–700	Midtown Tunnel	**36–38**
352–391	188–217	5–35	240–283	508–541	622–659	599–626	**34–36**
320–351	152–184	1–4	196–239	470–507	585–621	556–598	**32–34**
284–319	118–150	444–470	160–195	432–469	543–581	**Kips Bay**	**30–32**
250–283	79–117	404–431	120–159	394–431	500–541	**NYU Hosp.**	**28–30**
213–249	50–78	364–403	81–119	358–393	462–499	446–478	**26–28**
201–212	11–37	323–361	40–77	321–355	422–461	411–445	**24–26**
172–200	1–7	286–322	9–39	282–318	382–421	390–410	**22–24**
154–170		251–285	1–8	244–281	344–381	315–389	**20–22**
109–153		221–250	70–78	206–243	310–343	310–314	**18–20**
85–127		184–220	40–69	166–205	301–309	280–309	**16–18**
69–108		Union Square	2–30	126–165	230–240	240–279	**14–16**

Park Ave. / Park Ave. S. / Lexington Ave. / Irving Pl.

Fifth Ave. | Madison Ave. | Park Ave. | Lexington Ave. | Third Ave. | Second Ave. | First Ave.

1 → | **100** → | **140** → | **200** → | **300** → | **400** →

MAP 8 Streetfinder/The Village & Downtown

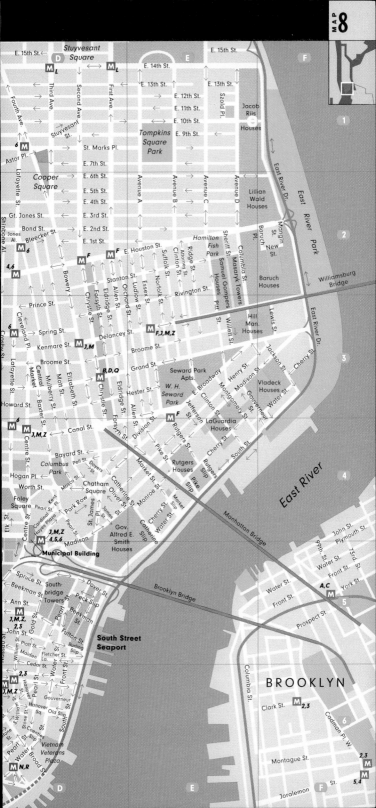

MAP 8

Streetfinder/The Village & Downtown

Letter codes refer to grid sectors on preceding map

Abingdon Sq. B1
Albany St. B6, C5
Allen St. D2, D3

Ann St. C5, D5
Astor Pl. D1
Attorney St. E2
Ave. A E1, E2
Ave. B E1, E2
Ave. C E1, E2
Ave. D E1, E2
Ave. of the Americas (Sixth Ave.) C1, C4
Bank St. A2, B1
Barclay St. C5
Barrow St. B2
Baruch Pl. F2
Battery Pl. C6
Baxter St. D3, D4
Bayard St. D4
Beach St. B4
Beaver St. C6, D6
Bedford St. B2, C2
Beekman St. D5
Bethune St. A1, B1
Bleecker St. B1, D2
Bond St. D2
Bowery D2, D4
Bowling Green C6
Bridge St. C6, D6
Broadway C1, C6
Brooklyn Battery Tunnel C6, D6
Brooklyn Bridge D5, F5
Broome St. B3, E3
Burling Slip D5
Canal St. C3, E3
Cardinal Hayes Plaza D4
Carlisle St. C6
Carmine St. B2
Catherine La. C4
Catherine Slip E4
Catherine St. D4, E4
Cedar St. C5, D5
Central Market D3
Centre St. D3, D5
Chambers St. B4, D4
Charles St. B1, B2

Charlton St. B3, C3
Chatham Sq. D4
Cherry St. E4, F3
Christopher St. B2, C1
Chrystie St. D2, D3
Church St. C4, C5
Clarkson St. B2, B3
Cleveland Pl. D3
Clinton St. E2, E4
Coenties Slip D6
Columbia St. E2, E3
Commerce St. B2
Cooper Sq. D1, D2
Cornelia St. B2
Cortlandt St. C5
Crosby St. C2, C3
Delancey St. D3, E3
Depyster St. D6
Desbrosses St. B3
Dey St. C5
Division St. D4, E4
Dominick St. B3, C3
Dover St. D5
Downing St. B2, C2
Doyers St. D4
Duane St. C4, D4
East Broadway D4, E3
East Houston St. D2, F2
East River Drive F1, F3
East Washington Pl. C2
Eighth Ave. B1
Eldridge St. D2, D3
Elizabeth St. D2, D4
Elk St. D4
Ericsson Pl. C4
Essex St. E2, E3
Exchange Pl. C6, D6
FDR Dr. F1, F3
Father Demo Sq. C2
Federal Plaza C4, D4
Fifth Ave. C1
First Ave. D1, D2
Fletcher St. D5
Foley Sq. D4
Forsyth St. D4, E4
Fourth Ave. D1
Franklin St. C4

Front St. D6
Fulton St. C5, D5
Gansevoort St. A1, B1
Gay St. B1, C1
Gold St. D5
Gouverneur La. D6
Gouverneur St. E3
Grand St. C3, F3
Great Jones St. D2
Greene St. C1, C3
Greenwich Ave. B1, C1
Greenwich St. B1, C6
Grove St. B2
Hanover Sq. D6
Hanover St. D6
Harrison St. B4, C4
Henry St. D4, E3
Hester St. D3, E3
Hogan Pl. D4
Holland Tunnel A4, C3
Horatio St. A1, B1
Hubert St. B4
Hudson St. B1, C4
Independence Plaza B4, C4
Jackson St. F3
James St. D4
Jane St. A1, B1
Jay St. C4
Jefferson St. E3
John St. C5, D5
Jones Alley D2
Jones St. B2
Kenmare St. D3
Kent Pl. D4
King St. B3, C3
Lafayette St. D1, D4
LaGuardia Pl. C2
Laight St. B4
Leonard St. C4
Leroy St. B2
Lewis St. F3
Liberty St. C5
Lispenard St. C4
Little W. 12th St. A1
Ludlow St. E2, E3
MacDougal Alley C1
MacDougal St. C1, C3

MAP 8

Letter codes refer to grid sectors on preceding map

MAP 9

Hospitals & Late-Night Pharmacies

MAP 9

Listed Alphabetically

HOSPITALS

Babies Hospital, 3. 622 W 168th St
☎ 305-2500

Beekman Downtown, 44. 170 William
St ☎ 312-5000

Bellevue Med Center, 33. 462 First
Ave ☎ 562-4141

Beth Israel Med Center, 36.
281 First Ave ☎ 420-2000

Beth Israel North, 13.
170 East End Ave ☎ 870-9000

Cabrini Med Center, 37. 227 E 19th St
☎ 995-6000

Coler Memorial, 14. Roosevelt Island
☎ 848-6000

Columbia Presbyterian, 1.
622 W 168th St ☎ 305-2500

Cooke Health Care Center, 9.
1249 Fifth Ave ☎ 360-1000

Cornell Med Center, 21. 525 E 68th
St ☎ 746-5454

Eye, Ear, & Throat, 24. 210 E 64th St
☎ 838-9200

Goldwater Memorial, 31.
Roosevelt Island ☎ 318-8000

Gouverneurs, 43. 227 Madison St
☎ 238-7000

Gracie Square, 20. 421 E 75th St
☎ 988-4400

Harkness Eye Institute, 5.
630 W 165th St ☎ 305-2500

Harlem Hospital Center, 6.
506 Lenox Ave ☎ 939-1000

Joint Diseases, 35. 301 E 17th St
☎ 598-6000

Lenox Hill, 16. 100 E 77th St
☎ 434-2000

Medical Arts Center, 25. 57 W 57th
St ☎ 755-0200

Metropolitan, 11. 1901 First Ave
☎ 423-6262

Mount Sinai, 10. 1 Gustav Levi Pl
☎ 241-6500

Nicolas Institute (Sports), 17.
100 E 77th St ☎ 434-2000

NY Orthopedic, 2. 622 W 168th St
☎ 305-2500

NYU Med Center, 32. 550 First Ave
☎ 263-7300

Payne Whitney (Psychiatric), 18.
420 E76th St ☎ 746-3800

Roosevelt, 26. 428 W 59th St
☎ 523-4000

Sloane (Women), 4.
622 W 168th St ☎ 305-5222

Sloane-Kettering (Cancer), 23. 1275
York Ave ☎ 639-2000

Special Surgery, 22. 535 E 70th St
☎ 606-1000

St Clare's, 28. 415 W 51st St
☎ 586-1500

St Luke's, 8. 419 W 114th St
☎ 523-4000

St Vincent's, 39. 153 W 11th St
☎ 604-7000

Strang Center, 19. 428 E 72nd
☎ 794-4900

**Sydenham (Neighborhood Family
Care Center), 7.** 215 W 125th St
☎ 932-6500

Veterans Admin, 34. 408 First Ave
☎ 686-7500

LATE-NIGHT PHARMACIES

Bigelow Pharmacy, 40. 414 Sixth Ave
☎ 533-2700

Chung Wah Pharmacy, 42. 65 Mott
St ☎ 587-4160

CVS Pharmacy, 38. 272 Eighth Ave
☎ 255-2592

Irmat Pharmacy, 12. 531 Columbus
Ave ☎ 362-2350

Kaufman Pharmacy, 30.
557 Lexington Ave ☎ 755-2266

Metropolis Drug Co, 29. 721 Ninth
Ave ☎ 246-0168

Pollack-Bailey Pharmacy, 27.
405 E 57th St ☎ 355-6094

Star Pharmacy, 15. 1540 First Ave
☎ 737-4324

Village Apothecary, 41. 346
Bleecker St ☎ 807-7566

MAP 10
Universities, Colleges & Schools

MAP 10

Listed Alphabetically

American Academy of Dramatic Arts, 30. 120 Madison Ave ☎ 686-9244

Art Students' League, 25. 215 W 57th St ☎ 247-4510

Bank St College, 11. 610 W 112th St ☎ 875-4400

Barnard College, 7. 3009 Broadway & 120th St ☎ 854-5262

Baruch College, 32. 17 Lexington Ave ☎ 802-2000

Cardozo Law, 34. 55 Fifth Ave ☎ 790-0200

Circle in the Square, 27. 1633 Broadway ☎ 307-2732

City College of NY, 3. Convent Ave & 138th St ☎ 650-7000

CUNY Graduate Sch and Univ Ctr, 28. 33 W 42nd St ☎ 642-1600

Columbia Physicians/Surgeons, 2. 630 W 168th St ☎ 305-3497

Columbia School of Social Work, 10. 622 W 113th St ☎ 854-4088

Columbia University, 8. B'way & 116th St ☎ 854-1754

Cooper Union, 37. 30 Cooper Sq ☎ 254-6300

Cornell Medical Center, 18. 1300 York Ave ☎ 746-5454

Fashion Institute of Technology, 31. 227 W 27th St ☎ 760-7675

Fordham University School of Law, 24. 140 W 62nd St ☎ 636-6890

Fordham University, 23. 113 W 60th St ☎ 636-6000

The French Culinary Institute, 44. 462 B'way ☎ 219-8890

Hebrew Union, 39. 1 W 4th St ☎ 674-5300

Hunter College, 17. 695 Park Ave ☎ 772-4000

Jewish Theological Seminary, 5. Broadway & 122nd St ☎ 678-8000

John Jay College, 26. 445 W 59th St ☎ 237-8000

Juilliard School of Music, 21. Lincoln Center, 144 W 66th St ☎ 799-5000

Leonard N. Stern School of Business at NYU, 38. 44 W 4th St ☎ 998-0100

Manhattan School of Music, 4. 120 Claremont Ave ☎ 749-2802

Mannes College of Music, 13. 150 W 85th St ☎ 580-0210

Martha Graham School, 20. 316 E 63rd St ☎ 838-5886

Marymount College, 14. 221 E 71st St ☎ 517-0400

Mount Sinai School of Medicine, 12. Fifth Ave & 100th St ☎ 241-6696

New School, 36. 66 W 12th St ☎ 229-5600

NY Institute of Technology, 16. 1855 Broadway ☎ 261-1500

NY Law School, 45. 57 Worth St ☎ 431-2100

NY School of Interior Design, 15. 170 E 70th St ☎ 753-5365

NYU, 41. Washington Sq ☎ 998-1212

NYU Law School, 40. 110 W 3rd St ☎ 998-6060

NYU Medical Center, 29. 550 First Ave ☎ 263-5290

Pace University, 46. 1 Pace Plaza ☎ 346-1200

Parsons School of Design, 35. 66 Fifth Ave ☎ 229-8900

Pratt Institute, 43. 259 Lafayette St ☎ 925-8481

Rockefeller University, 19. York Ave & 66th St ☎ 327-8000

School of American Ballet, 22. 165 W 65th St ☎ 877-0600

School of Visual Arts, 33. 209 E 23rd St ☎ 679-7350

Stella Adler Conservatory, 42. 419 Lafayette St ☎ 260-0525

Teachers College, 9. 525 W 120th St ☎ 678-3000

Union Theological Seminary, 6. Broadway & 120th St ☎ 662-7100

Yeshiva University, 1. Amsterdam Ave & 185th St ☎ 960-5400

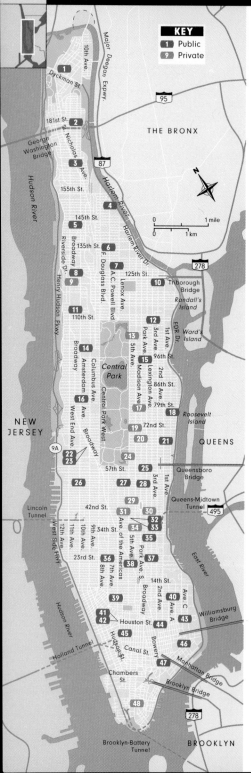

MAP 11 | Libraries

MAP 11

Listed Alphabetically

PUBLIC

Aguila, 12. 1955 3rd Ave ☎ 534-2930

Andrew Heiskell Library For the Blind and Physically Handicapped, 38. 40 W 20th St ☎ 206-5400

Bloomingdale, 14. 150 W 100th St ☎ 222-8030

Cathedrale, 28. 560 Lexington Ave ☎ 752-3824

Chatham Square, 47. 33 E Broadway ☎ 964-6598

Columbia Univ, 11. 521 W 114th St ☎ 864-2530

Columbus, 26. 742 Tenth Ave ☎ 586-5098

Countee Cullen, 7. 104 W 136th St ☎ 491-2070

Donnell, 27. 20 W 53rd St ☎ 621-0618

Early Childhood, 41. 66 Leroy St ☎ 929-0815

Epiphany, 37. 228 E 23rd St ☎ 679-2645

58th St, 25. 127 E 58th St ☎ 759-7358

Fort Washington, 2. 535 W 179th St ☎ 927-3533

George Bruce, 8. 518 W 125th St ☎ 662-9727

Hamilton Fish Park, 43. 415 E Houston St ☎ 673-2290

Hamilton Grange, 5. 503 W 145th St ☎ 926-2147

Hudson Park, 42. 66 Leroy St ☎ 243-6876

Inwood, 1. 4790 Broadway ☎ 942-2445

Jefferson Market, 39. 425 Sixth Ave ☎ 243-4334

Kips Bay, 35. 446 Third Ave ☎ 683-2520

Lincoln Center, 23. 111 Amsterdam Ave ☎ 870-1630

Macomb's Bridge, 4. 2650 Seventh Ave ☎ 281-4900

Mid-Manhattan, 33. 455 Fifth Ave ☎ 340-0849

Muhlenberg, 36. 209 W 23rd St ☎ 924-1585

NY Public (Main), 32. Fifth Ave & 42nd St ☎ 930-0800

96th St, 15. 112 E 96th St ☎ 289-0908

125th St, 10. 224 E 125th St ☎ 534-5050

Ottendorfer, 45. 135 Second Ave ☎ 674-0947

Riverside, 22. 127 Amsterdam Ave ☎ 870-1810

St Agnes, 16. 444 Amsterdam Ave ☎ 877-4380

Schomburg Center, 6. 515 W 135th St ☎ 491-2200

Seward Park, 46. 192 E Broadway ☎ 477-6770

67th St, 21. 328 E 67th St ☎ 734-1717

Tompkins Square, 40. 331 E 10th St ☎ 228-4747

Washington Heights, 3. 1000 St Nicholas Ave ☎ 923-6054

Webster, 18. 1465 York Ave ☎ 288-5049

PRIVATE

Alliance Francaise, 24. 22 E 60th St ☎ 355-6100

Archive of Contemporary Music, 44. 132 Crosby ☎ 226-6967

Frick Art, 19. 10 E 71st St ☎ 288-8700

Goethe House, 30. 1014 Fifth Ave ☎ 439-8700

Italian Institute, 20. 686 Park Ave ☎ 879-4242

Jewish Theological Seminary, 9. 3080 Broadway ☎ 678-8080

Mercantile, 29. 17 E 47th St ☎ 755-6710

NY Academy of Medicine, 13. 2 E 103rd St ☎ 876-8200

NY Bar Association, 31. 42 W 44th St ☎ 382-6600

NY Law, 48. 120 Broadway ☎ 732-8720

NY Society, 17. 53 E 79th St ☎ 288-6900

Pierpont Morgan, 34. 29 E 36th St ☎ 685-0008

MAP 12
Consulates & Missions

Great Lawn

Belvedere Lake

79th St. Transverse

E. 81st St.

E. 80th St.

1

Metropolitan Museum of Art

3

E. 79th St.

2

Third Ave.

Second Ave.

First Ave.

York Ave.

Central Park

E. 78th St.

E. 77th St.

4 **5**

6

E. 76th St.

6 M

Lenox Hill Hospital

E. 75th St.

The Lake

7

Whitney Museum

E. 74th St.

Lexington Ave.

E. 73rd St.

8

Fifth Ave.

Madison Ave.

Park Ave.

9

E. 72nd St.

Frick Collection

10

E. 71st St.

York Ave.

11

E. 70th St.

Hunter College

E. 69th St.

12

E. 68th St.

6 M

The Mall

Catherines Park

13

E. 67th St.

14

E. 66th St.

17 **16**

Sheep Meadow

E. 65th St.

65th St. Transverse

E. 64th St.

18

15

Central Park Wildlife Conservation Center

E. 63rd St.

B,Q M

Wollman Rink

Children's Zoo

E. 62nd St.

E. 61st St.

The Pond

E. 60th St.

4,5,6, N,R M

TRAMWAY TO ROOSEVELT ISLAND

19

Central Park South

Grand Army Plaza

N,R M

E. 59th St.

21

20

Queensboro Br.

W. 58th St.

E. 58th St.

Sutton Place

N,R M

B,Q M

E. 57th St.

22

Carnegie Hall

E. 56th St.

Third Ave.

Second Ave.

First Ave.

23

E. 55th St.

Park Ave.

24

E,F M

E. 54th St.

E,F M

E. 53rd St.

B,D,E M

25 **26**

27

32 **28**

33 **29**

E. 52nd St.

35

30

31

34 **6**

E. 51st St.

36

W. 50th St.

B,D,F,Q M

Rockefeller Center

St. Patrick's Cathedral

E. 50th St.

42

37

38

Beekman Pl.

39

40

N,R M

45

46

41

44

48

49

W. 48th St.

47

E. 49th St.

43

58

W. 47th St.

50

E. 48th St.

55

51

Duffy Square

W. 46th St.

56 **57**

E. 47th St.

52

53

54

59

Ave. of the Americas

W. 45th St.

E. 46th St.

60

Times Square

W. 44th St.

Fifth Ave.

Madison Ave.

Vanderbilt Ave.

Grand Central Terminal

E. 45th St.

64 **63**

62

61

72

W. 43rd St.

N.Y. Public Library (Main)

E. 44th St.

65

66

67

UN Plaza

UN Headquarters

B,D, F,Q M

Chrysler Building

68

69

71 **70**

1,2,3,7,9 N,R,S, M

W. 41st St.

73

Bryant Park

E. 42nd St.

4,5, 6,7 M

Queens-Midtown Tunnel

Seventh Ave.

W. 40th St.

76 **77**

E. 41st St.

81

82

78 **79**

E. 40th St.

W. 39th St.

(Sixth Ave.)

75

88

87

E. 39th St.

83

84 **85**

FDR Dr.

W. 38th St.

E. 38th St.

80

93

92

W. 37th St.

91

W. 36th St.

90

E. 36th St.

Park Ave.

89

86

Island 34 St. East Heliport

74

Herald Square

E. 35th St.

Empire State Building

E. 34th St.

B,D,F, N,Q,R M

1,2,3,9 M

Second Ave.

MAP **12**

Listed by Site Number

1 Czech	47 Japan	70 Tanzania
2 Greece	48 Afghanistan	71 Croatia
3 Iraq	48 Chile	72 Dominican
4 Mongolia	48 Ethiopia	Republic
5 Myanmar	48 Finland	73 China
6 Lebanon	48 Guyana	74 Costa Rica
7 France	48 Jordan	74 Honduras
8 Cameroon	48 Oman	75 Haiti
9 Burkina Faso	48 Panama	76 Mexico
10 Italy	48 Saudi Arabia	77 Gabon
11 Austria	48 Yemen	78 Morocco
12 Indonesia	49 Slovakia	79 Cyprus
13 Senegal	50 Gambia	80 Lithuania
14 Belarus	50 Ghana	81 Sri Lanka
14 Russia	51 Slovenia	82 Iran
14 Ukraine	51 Sweden	83 Lesotho
15 Palestine Liberation	52 Qatar	84 Romania
Organization (PLO)	52 United Arab	85 South Africa
16 Congo	Emirates	86 Malta
17 Pakistan	52 Uruguay	87 Cuba
18 India	53 Sudan	88 Guinea
19 Somalia	53 Sudan	89 Paraguay
20 Egypt	53 Trinidad & Tobago	90 El Salvador
21 Spain	54 Bahamas	91 Botswana
22 Germany	55 Jamaica	92 Guatemala
22 Korea	56 Philippines	93 Poland
23 Argentina	57 Colombia	
24 Belgium	58 Denmark	
25 Hungary	59 Bangladesh	
26 Zambia	59 Turkey	
27 Thailand	60 USA	
28 Switzerland	61 Bahrain	
29 Venezuela	61 Bhutan	
30 Canada	62 Fiji	
31 Belgium	62 New Zealand	
32 Australia	62 Surinam	
32 Estonia	63 Kuwait	
33 Brazil	64 Nigeria	
33 Portugal	65 Grenada	
34 Ireland	65 Liberia	
35 Laos	65 Nepal	
36 Great Britain	65 Nicaragua	
36 Monaco	65 St Lucia	
37 Norway	65 Syria	
38 Niger	66 Malaysia	
39 Tunisia	67 Barbados	
40 Luxembourg	67 Equador	
41 Iceland	67 Israel	
42 Peru	68 Bolivia	
43 New Zealand	68 Mauritania	
44 Sierra Leone	68 Mauritius	
45 Netherlands	69 Madagascar	
46 Kenya	69 St Vincent	

MAP 12

Consulates & Missions

Listed Alphabetically

CONSULATES

Argentina, 23. 12 W 56th St ☎ 603-0400

Australia, 32. 630 Fifth Ave ☎ 408-8400

Austria, 11. 31 E 69th St ☎ 737-6400

Bahamas, 54. 231 E 46th St ☎ 421-6420

Bahrain, 61. 2 UN Plaza ☎ 223-6200

Bangladesh, 59. 821 UN Plaza ☎ 867-3434

Barbados, 67. 800 Second Ave ☎ 867-8431

Belgium, 31. 1330 Avenue of the Americas ☎ 586-5110

Bhutan, 61. 2 UN Plaza ☎ 826-1919

Bolivia, 68. 211 E 43rd St ☎ 687-0530

Brazil, 33. 630 Fifth Ave ☎ 757-3085

Canada, 30. 1251 Sixth Ave ☎ 596-1700

Chile, 48. 866 UN Plaza ☎ 980-3366

China, 73. 520 Twelfth Ave ☎ 868-7752

Colombia, 57. 10 E 46th St ☎ 949-9898

Costa Rica, 74. 80 Wall St ☎ 425-2620

Cyprus, 79. 13 E 40th St ☎ 686-6016

Denmark, 58. 835 Second Ave ☎ 223-4545

Dominican Republic, 72. 1 Times Sq ☎ 768-2480

Ecuador, 67. 800 Second Ave ☎ 808-0170

Egypt, 20. 1110 Second Ave ☎ 759-7120

El Salvador, 90. 46 Park Ave ☎ 889-3608

Estonia, 32. 630 Fifth Ave ☎ 247-7634

Fiji, 62. 1 UN Plaza ☎ 355-7316

Finland, 48. 866 UN Plaza ☎ 750-4400

France, 7. 934 Fifth Ave ☎ 606-3688

Germany, 22. 460 Park Ave ☎ 308-8700

Ghana, 50. 19 E 47th St ☎ 832-1300

Great Britain, 36. 845 Third Ave ☎ 745-0202

Greece, 2. 69 E 79th St ☎ 988-5500

Grenada, 65. 820 Second Ave ☎ 599-0301

Guatemala, 92. 57 Park Ave ☎ 686-3837

Guyana, 48. 866 UN Plaza ☎ 527-3215

Haiti, 75. 271 Madison Ave ☎ 697-9767

Honduras, 74. 80 Wall St ☎ 269-3611

Hungary, 25. 223 E 52nd St ☎ 752-0661

Iceland, 41. 800 Third Ave ☎ 593-2700

India, 18. 3 E 64th St ☎ 879-7800

Indonesia, 12. 5 E 68th St ☎ 879-0600

Ireland, 34. 345 Park Ave ☎ 319-2555

Israel, 67. 800 Second Ave ☎ 499-5000

Italy, 10. 690 Park Ave ☎ 737-9100

Jamaica, 55. 767 Third Ave ☎ 935-9000

Japan, 47. 299 Park Ave ☎ 371-8222

Kenya, 46. 424 Madison Ave ☎ 486-1300

Korea, 22. 460 Park Ave ☎ 752-1700

Kuwait, 63. 321 E 44th St ☎ 973-4318

Lebanon, 6. 9 E 76th St ☎ 744-7905

Liberia, 65. 820 Second Ave ☎ 687-1033

Lithuania, 80. 420 Fifth Ave ☎ 354-7840

Luxembourg, 40. 17 Beekman Pl ☎ 888-6664

Madagascar, 69. 801 Second Ave ☎ 986-9491

Malaysia, 66. 313 E 43rd St ☎ 490-2722

Mexico, 76. 8 E 41 St ☎ 689-0456

Monaco, 36. 845 Third Ave ☎ 759-5227

Morocco, 78. 10 E 40th St ☎ 758-2625

Nepal, 65. 820 Second Ave ☎ 370-4188

Netherlands, 45. 1 Rockefeller Plaza ☎ 246-1429

New Zealand, 43. 780 Third Ave ☎ 832-4038

Nigeria, 64. 828 Second Ave ☎ 808-0301

Norway, 37. 825 Third Ave ☎ 421-7333

Pakistan, 17. 12 E 65th St ☎ 879-5800

Paraguay, 89. 300 E 40th St ☎ 682-9441

Peru, 42. 215 Lexington Ave ☎ 481-7410

Philippines, 56. 556 Fifth Ave ☎ 764-1300

Poland, 93. 233 Madison Ave ☎ 889-8360

MAP 12

Listed Alphabetically (cont.)

Portugal, 33. 630 Fifth Ave
☎ 765–2980

Saudi Arabia, 48. 866 UN Plaza
☎ 752–2740

South Africa, 85. 333 E 38th St
☎ 213–4880

Spain, 21. 150 E 58th St ☎ 355–4080

Sri Lanka, 81. 630 Third Ave
☎ 986–7040

Sweden, 51. 1 Dag Hammarskjold
Plaza ☎ 751–5900

Switzerland, 28. 665 Fifth Ave
☎ 758–2560

Thailand, 27. 351 E 52nd St
☎ 754–1770

Trinidad & Tobago, 53. 733 Third
Ave ☎ 682–7272

Turkey, 59. 821 UN Plaza ☎ 949–0160

Uruguay, 52. 747 Third Ave
☎ 753–8191

Venezuela, 29. 7 E 51st St
☎ 826–1660

Yemen, 48. 866 UN Plaza
☎ 355–1730

MISSIONS

Afghanistan, 48. 866 UN Plaza
☎ 754–1191

Belarus, 14. 136 E 67th St ☎ 535–3420

Botswana, 91. 103 E 37th St
☎ 889–2277

Burkina Faso, 9. 115 E 73rd St
☎ 288–7515

Cameroon, 8. 22 E 73rd St
☎ 794–2295

Congo, 16. 14 E 65th St ☎ 744–7840

Croatia, 71. 201 E 42nd St
☎ 986–1585

Cuba, 87. 315 Lexington Ave
☎ 689–7215

Czech Republic, 1.
1109 Madison Ave ☎ 535–8814

Ethiopia, 48. 866 UN Plaza
☎ 421–1830

Gabon, 77. 18 E 41st St ☎ 686–9720

Gambia, 50. 820 Second Ave
☎ 949–6640

Guinea, 88. 140 E 39th St ☎ 687–8115

Iran, 82. 622 Third Ave ☎ 687–2020

Iraq, 3. 14 E 79th St ☎ 737–4433

Jordan, 48. 866 UN Plaza
☎ 752–0135

Laos, 35. 317 E 51st St ☎ 832–2734

Lesotho, 83. 204 E 39th St
☎ 661–1690

Malta, 86. 249 E 35th St
☎ 725–2345

Mauritania, 68. 211 E 43rd St
☎ 986–7963

Mauritius, 68. 211 E 43rd St
☎ 949–0190

Mongolia, 4. 6 E 77th St ☎ 861–9460

Myanmar, 5. 10 E 77th St ☎ 535–1310

New Zealand, 62. 1 UN Plaza
☎ 826–1960

Nicaragua, 65. 820 Second Ave
☎ 490–7997

Niger, 38. 417 E 50th St ☎ 421–3260

Oman, 48. 866 UN Plaza
☎ 355–3505

Panama, 48. 866 UN Plaza
☎ 421–5420

**Palestine Liberation Organization
(PLO), 15.** 115 E 65th St ☎ 288–8500

Qatar, 52. 747 Third Ave ☎ 486–9335

Republic of Slovakia, 49.
866 UN Plaza ☎ 980–1558

Romania, 84. 202 E 38th St
☎ 682–3274

Russia Federation, 14. 136 E 67th St
☎ 861–4900

Senegal, 13. 238 E 68th St
☎ 517–9030

Sierra Leone, 44. 245 E 49th St
☎ 688–1656

Slovenia, 51. 1 Dag Hammarskjold
Plaza ☎ 370–3007

Somalia, 19. 425 E 61st St
☎ 688–9410

St Lucia, 65. 820 Second Ave
☎ 697–9360

St Vincent, 69. 801 Second Ave
☎ 687–4490

Sudan, 53. 733 Third Ave
☎ 573–6033

Surinam, 62. 1 UN Plaza ☎ 826–0660

Syria, 65. 820 Second Ave
☎ 661–1313

Tanzania, 70. 205 E 42nd St
☎ 972–9160

Tunisia, 39. 31 Beekman Plaza
☎ 751–7503

Ukraine, 14. 136 E 67th St
☎ 535–3418

United Arab Emirates, 52.
747 Third Ave ☎ 371–0480

USA, 60. 799 UN Plaza ☎ 415–4000

Zambia, 26. 237 E 52nd St
☎ 758–1110

MAP **13** **Airport Access**

Airline Terminals

AIRLINES	JFK	LaGUARDIA	NEWARK
Aer Lingus ☎ 212/557-1110	EWD		
Aerolineas Argentinas ☎ 800/333-0276	EWD (Iberia)		
Aeroflot ☎ 212/332-1050	Delta Terminal		
AeroMexico ☎ 800/237-6639	EWD		Terminal B
Air Afrique ☎ 800/237-2747	WWD (Air France)		
Air Alliance ☎ 800/776-3000			Terminal C
Air Aruba ☎ 800/882-7822			Terminal B
Air Canada ☎ 800/776-3000		CTB	Terminal C
Air China ☎ 212/371-9898	Delta Terminal		
Air France ☎ 800/237-2747	WWD		Terminal B
Air India ☎ 212/751-6200	WWD		
Air Jamaica ☎ 800/523-5585	EWD (Alitalia)		
Air Nova ☎ 800/776-3000			Terminal C
Air Ontario ☎ 800/776-3000			Terminal C
Alitalia ☎ 800/223-5730	WWD		Terminal C
ALIA-Royal Jordanian ☎ 212/949-0050	EWD		
All Nippon Airways ☎ 800/235-9262	Delta Terminal		
American ☎ 800/433-7300	American/3	CTB	Terminal A
American Eagle ☎ 800/433-7300	Terminal 3		
America West ☎ 800/235-9292	Delta Terminal	CTB	Terminal C
Asiana Airlines ☎ 212/227-4262	EWD (Aer Lingus)		
Austrian Airlines ☎ 800/843-0002	Delta Terminal		
Avensa ☎ 800/428-3672	EWD (Iberia)		
Avianca ☎ 212/399-0800	DeltaTerminal		
Balkan Bulgarian ☎ 212/371-2047	EWD		
British Airways ☎ 800/247-9297	American		Terminal B
Business Express ☎ 800/345-3400	Delta Terminal	Delta Terminal	Terminal B
BWIA ☎ 800/327-7401	British Airways		
Carnival ☎ 800/437-2110	TWA Terminal 4B		Terminal B
China Airlines ☎ 800/227-5118	EWD (Iberia)		
Colgan Air ☎ 800/272-5488		CTB	Terminal A
Continental ☎ 800/525-0280		CTB	Terminal C

MAP 13

Airline Terminals (cont.)

AIRLINES	JFK	LaGUARDIA	NEWARK
Continental Express ☎ 800/525-0280			Terminal C
Czechoslovak ☎ 212/765-6022	Terminal 1A		
Delta International ☎ 212/239-0700	Delta Terminal	Delta Terminal	Terminal B
Delta Domestic ☎ 201/622-2111	Delta Terminal	Delta Terminal	Terminal B
Delta Shuttle ☎ 212/239-0700		MAT	
Ecuatoriana ☎ 800/328-2367	TWA Terminal 4B		
El-Al ☎ 212/768-9200	WWD		
EVA Airways ☎ 800/695-1188			Terminal B
Egypt Air ☎ 212/315-0900	WWD (Alitalia)		
Finnair ☎ 212/889-7070	American Airlines		
Guyana ☎ 718/657-7474	EWD		
Hispaniola ☎ 305/591-1704	WWD		
Iberia ☎ 800/772-4642	EWD		
Icelandair ☎ 718/917-0640	EWD		
Japan ☎ 212/838-4400	EWD		
KIWI ☎ 800/538-5494			Terminal A
KLM ☎ 212/759-3600; 800/374-7747	EWD		
Korean ☎ 800/223-1155	WWD		
Kuwait ☎ 212/308-5454	EWD (Lufthansa)		
Ladeco ☎ 718/244-6281; 800/825-2332	EWD (Icelandair)		
Lacsa Airlines ☎ 800/225-2272	EWD		
Lan Chile ☎ 800/735-5526	British Airways Terminal 5		
Leisure Air ☎ 212/268-7733	Terminal 1		
Long Island ☎ 516/752-8300		MAT	
LOT Polish ☎ 800/223-0593	WWD (Air France)		Terminal B
LTU ☎ 800/888-0200	EWD (KLM)		
Lufthansa ☎ 800/645-3880	EWD		Terminal B
Malev ☎ 212/757-6480; 800/223-6884			Terminal B
Mexicana ☎ 800/531-7921			Terminal B
Midwest Express ☎ 800/452-2022		CTB	Terminal B
Nigeria ☎ 212/935-2700	WWD		

MAP 14 New York Area Airports

JFK International Airport

Airline Terminals (cont.)

AIRLINES	JFK	LaGUARDIA	NEWARK
North American ☎ 718/656-3289	TWA Terminal B	Delta Terminal	Terminal B
Northwest International ☎ 800/447-4747	EWD (KLM)	Delta Terminal	Terminal B
Northwest Domestic ☎ 800/225-2525		Delta`Terminal	Terminal B
Northwest Airlink ☎ 800/225-2525	EWD (KLM)		
Olympic ☎ 212/838-3600	EWD (Lufthansa)		
Pakistan ☎ 212/370-9158	WWD		
Philippine Airlines ☎ 800/435-9725	TWA Terminal 4B		
Qantas ☎ 800/227-4500	American Airlines		
Royal Air Maroc ☎ 212/750-6071	EWD (Lufthansa)		
SAS ☎ 800/221-2350			Terminal C
Sabena ☎ 800/955-2000	American Airlines		
SAETA ☎ 800/827-2382	British Airways		
Singapore Airlines ☎ 800/742-3333	Delta Terminal		
South African Airways ☎ 212/826-0995	American Airlines		
Surinam Airways ☎ 800/327-6864	Terminal 1		
Swissair ☎ 800/221-4750	Delta Terminal		
Tarom-Romanian ☎ 212/687-6013	Terminal 1A		
TACA International ☎ 800/535-8780	WWD (Air India)		
TAP Air Portugal ☎ 800/221-7370	EWD (Lufthansa)		Terminal B
Tower Air ☎ 718/553-8500	Terminal 1		
TransBrasil ☎ 800/872-3153	TWA Terminal 4B		
TWA ☎ 212/290-2141; 201/643-3339	TWA Int'l & Dom.	CTB	Terminal A
Turkish Airlines ☎ 718/244-7760			Terminal B
TW Express ☎ 212/290-2141;201/643-3339	TWA Terminal 4A		Terminal A
United ☎ 800/241-6522	British Airways	CTB	Terminal A
United Express ☎ 800/241-6522	British Airways		Terminal A
USAir ☎ 800/428-4322	TWA Terminal 4A	USAir Terminal	Terminal A
USAir Express ☎ 800/428-4322	TWA Terminal 4A	USAir Terminal	Terminal A
USAir Shuttle ☎ 800/428-4322		USAir Shuttle Ter	
Varig ☎ 212/682-3100	EWD		
Virgin Atlantic ☎ 800/862-8621	WWD (Air France)		Terminal A

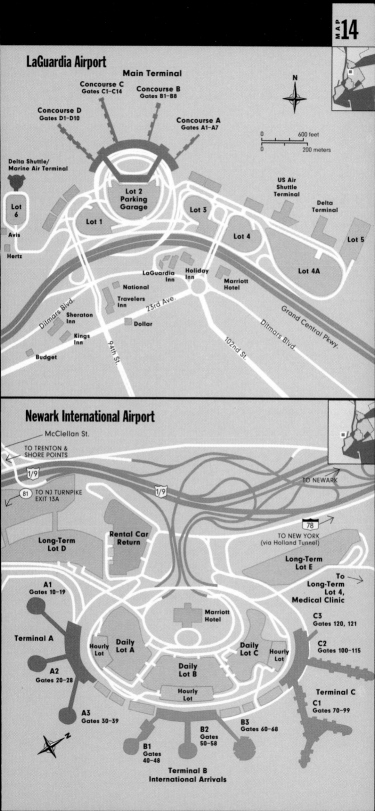

MAP 15 Passenger Rail Network

PORT JERVIS LINE

Sloatsburg

Spring Valley

N E W

Suffern

ROCKLAND

Mahwah

Nanuet

Pearl River

Ramsey

Montvale
Park Ridge
Woodcliff Lake

MAIN LINE

Allendale

Hillsdale

Waldwick

Westwood

Ho-Ho-Kus

B E R G E N

PASCACK VALLEY LINE

Ridgewood

Glen Rock   Glen Rock

Emerson

BERGEN LINE

River Edge

Hawthorne

Radburn

North Hackensack

P A S S A I C

MAIN LINE

Lincoln Park   Mountain View/Wayne

Broadway/Fairlawn

Towaco

Paterson

Plauderville

Anderson St.

N E W   J E R S E Y

Boonton

Little Falls

Clifton

Garfield

Essex St.

Mountain Lakes

Great Notch
Montclair Heights
Mountain Ave.
Upper Montclair
Watchung Ave.
Walnut St.

Passaic

Teterboro

BOONTON LINE

Wood-Ridge

Mount Tabor

Delawanna

Rutherford

Morris Plains

Montclair

Glen Ridge
Bloomfield

Lyndhurst

MORRISTOWN LINE

E S S E X

Glen Ridge
Bloomfield

Kingsland

Grand Central Terminal
Penn Station

Morristown

Harmon Cove

MORRISTOWN LINE

MONTCLAIR BRANCH

Watsessing

Arlington

Convent Station

Orange
Highland Ave.
Mountain Station
South Orange
Maplewood

Ampere

Hoboken

33rd St.

Madison

Newark

Pavonia

MANHATTAN

Chatham

Penn Station/Newark

World Trade Center

Summit

Millburn

Short Hills

Journal Square

Grove St.
Exchange Place

Murray Hill

New Providence

PATH

Flatbush Ave.

GLADSTONE BRANCH

U N I O N

North Elizabeth

H U D S O N

Upper New York Bay

Berkeley Heights

Cranford
Roselle Park

Elizabeth

St George

Garwood

Tompkinsville

Westfield

Stapleton

Fanwood

Linden

S T A T E N   I S L A N D

Clifton

Netherwood

North Rahway

Grasmere

Plainfield

Rahway

Old Town

Metropark

Dongan Hills

RARITAN VALLEY LINE

Avenel

Grant City

Jefferson Ave.

Dunellen

Woodbridge

Oakwood Heights

New Dorp

AMTRAK

Metuchen

Great Kills

Bay Terrace

Annandale

Eltingville

STATEN ISLAND RAPID TRANSIT

New Brunswick

Edison

Prince's Bay

Huguenot

Lower New York Bay

New Providence

Nassau

Pleasant Plains
Richmond Valley

NORTHEAST CORRIDOR LINE

Highland Park

Perth Amboy

Atlantic

Tottenville

Jersey Ave.

South Amboy

Raritan Bay

M I D D L E S E X

NORTH JERSEY COAST LINE

M O N M O U T H

Matawan   Hazlet   Middletown

MAP **15**

Ossining • Chappaqua • New Canaan •

Scarborough • Pleasantville • Talmadge Hill •

FAIRFIELD

YORK • Hawthorne • Springdale •

Mount Pleasant

Philipse Manor • Rowayton •

AMTRAK **HUDSON** Valhalla • Glenbrook • Darien •
LINE CONNECTICUT Noroton
Heights
Tarrytown • North White Plains • **AMTRAK** Stamford

Irvington • White Plains • Old Greenwich •

Ardsley • **HARLEM** Riverside •
LINE Cos Cob •
Dobbs Ferry • Hartsdale • Greenwich •

Scarsdale • Port Chester •
Hastings-on-
Hudson • WESTCHESTER Rye • **OYSTER BAY**
Crestwood • Harrison • **BRANCH**
Greystone • Tuckahoe • Mamaroneck • Mill Neck •
Glenwood • Bronxville •
Fleetwood • Mount Vernon • Long Island Sound Cold Spring
Mt. Vernon • W. • Larchmont • Harbor
Yonkers • Pelham • Locust Valley • ☐ **Oyster Bay**
Ludlow • **NEW HAVEN** Glen Cove •
New Rochelle **LINE** Glen St. •
Riverdale • Wakefield • **PORT JEFFERSON**
Spuyten Woodlawn • Sea Cliff • **BRANCH**
Duyvil • Glen Head •
Marble Williams Bridge **PORT WASHINGTON** Syosset •
Hill • Botanical Gardens **BRANCH**
University Heights • Fordham ☐ **Port** Greenvale •
Morris **AMTRAK** Washington
Heights • **BRONX** Plandome • **NASSAU**
Melrose • East Great Neck • Manhasset • Roslyn •
River Little Neck • Mineola •
125th • LaGuardia Bayside • Albertson • Hicksville • Bethpage •
St. Airport Douglaston • East
Auburndale • Williston • **RONKONKOMA**
Hunters Point Broadway New Hyde Park • Westbury **BRANCH**
Ave. • Woodside • Murray Hill Merrick Ave. • Carle Place •
Penny Flushing Nassau • Massapequa •
Bridge • Shea Stewart Country Garden City •
Haberman Stadium Forest Manor • Life Press Bellmore •
Long Island Fresh Pond Hills • Floral Park • **Hempstead** ☐ Seaford •
City • **QUEENS** Jamaica • Bellerose • **West** Merrick • Wantagh •
Glendale • Queens Hempstead Gdns • **Hempstead** Freeport •
Village • Lakeview Baldwin •
Nostrand Richmond St. Albans • Malverne • Rockville
Ave. • Hill Locust Hollis • Westwood • Center
Manor Lauralton Lyn- Center Ave.
East Rosedale • brook • East Rockaway
BROOKLYN New York Kennedy Valley Gibson Ocean Side •
International Stream •
Airport Hewlett •
Inwood • Woodmere •
Cedarhurst • Island Park •
Lawrence • ☐ **Long Beach**
Far
☐ Rockaway
BABYLON BRANCH/
MONTAUK BRANCH

ATLANTIC OCEAN

N

0 ___ 10 miles
0 _____ 15 km

KEY
▬ Amtrak
▬ Long Island Railroad
▬ Metro-North Commuter Railroad
▬ New Jersey Transit
▬ PATH (Port Authority Trans-Hudson)
▬ Staten Island Rapid Transit

Hudson River

MAP 16 **Piers & Terminals**

George Washington Bridge
Bus Terminal
(178th St.)

125th St.
Station

107th St.
Recreation Pier

The
Reservoir

W. 86th St.

E. 86th St.

West End Ave.

Amsterdam Ave.

Riverside Dr.

W. 79th St.

E. 79th St.

Riverside
Park

Roosevelt
Island

Hudson
Harbor/
79th St.
Boat Basin

Central
Park

Columbus Ave.

Broadway

W. 72nd St.

E. 72nd St.

Lexington Ave.

Third Ave.

Second Ave.

First Ave.

York Ave.

East River

LONG
ISLAND
CITY

UPPER
WEST
SIDE

Central Park W.

Fifth Ave.

Madison Ave.

Park Ave.

UPPER
EAST
SIDE

E. 65th St.

Vernon Blvd.

9A

E. 63rd St.
Ferry Landing

Central Park S.

E. 59th St.

TRAMWAY

W. 57th St.

E. 57th St.

Queensboro
Bridge

Ninth Ave.

Eighth Ave.

E. 53rd St.

QUEENS

W. 50th St.

TURTLE
BAY

MIDTOWN

Passenger
Ship
Terminal

THEATER
DISTRICT

Grand Central
Terminal

Pier 83

The Intrepid
Sea-Air-Space
Museum

W. 42nd St.

E. 42nd St.

495

495

Pier 78

Port Authority
Bus Terminal

MURRAY
HILL

Queens-Midtown
Tunnel

Lincoln
Tunnel

HELL'S
KITCHEN

Broadway

W. 34th St.

E. 34th St.

E. 34th St. Pier
NYC Heliport

Javits Center

Pennsylvania
Station

Ave. of the Americas

Seventh Ave.

Fifth Ave.

Madison Ave.

Park Ave.

Lexington Ave.

Third Ave.

Second Ave.

First Ave.

GREEN-
POINT

West 30th St.
Heliport

Eleventh Ave.

Tenth Ave.

Ninth Ave.

W. 23rd St.

E. 23rd St.

Pier 62

CHELSEA

Eighth Ave.

GRAMERCY
PARK

East
River

FDR Dr.

W. 14th St.

E. 14th St.

Fourth Ave.

PATH

PATH

PATH

Ave. A

Ave. B

Ave. C

Ave. D

Greenwich Ave.

PATH

GREENWICH
VILLAGE

EAST VILLAGE

NEW
JERSEY

WEST VILLAGE

(Sixth Ave.)

Lafayette

NOHO

Hudson River

PATH

Washington St.

W. Houston St.

Houston St.

E. Houston St.

Bowery

LOWER EAST SIDE

Williamsburg
Bridge

Hoboken
Terminal

PATH

Greenwich St.

West Side Hwy.

SOHO

Broadway

E. Broadway

HOBOKEN

Holland Tunnel

Varick St.

DOWNTOWN

LITTLE
ITALY

Canal St.

TRIBECA

Church St.

CHINATOWN

Manhattan
Bridge

JERSEY
CITY

PATH

Chambers St.

Brooklyn Bridge

278

N

PATH

BROOKLYN

New York Cove
Yacht Harbor

FINANCIAL
DISTRICT

South Street
Seaport

BROOKLYN
HEIGHTS

BATTERY
PARK
CITY

Wall St.

Pier 11

Brooklyn Queens Expwy.

Pier A

Downtown
Manhattan Heliport

Battery
Park

Staten Island
Ferry Terminal

Battery Park Ferry Landing
(Ferries to Statue of Liberty
and Ellis Island)

Slip 5

Brooklyn-Battery
Tunnel

0   1500 feet
0   500 meters

MAP 16

Listed Alphabetically

BOAT TOURS

Circle Line, Pier 83 ☎ 563-3200

Seaport Liberty Cruise, Pier 16 ☎ 748-8618

Spirit of New York, Pier 62 ☎ 727-2789

TNT Hydrolines, Pier 11 ☎ 800/262-8743

World Yacht Cruises, Pier 81 ☎ 630-8100

FERRY SERVICE

Ellis Island, Battery Park ☎ 269-5755

Hoboken (New Jersey), North Cove Harbor ☎ 201/420-4422

Delta Water Shuttle (to LaGuardia Airport), Pier 11 ☎ 800/543-3779

Port Imperial (to New Jersey), Pier 78 ☎ 201/902-8735

Port Liberty (to New Jersey), Pier 11 ☎ 201/433-1444

Staten Island, Battery Park ☎ 718/390-5253

Statue of Liberty, Battery Park ☎ 269-5755

HELICOPTER SERVICE

Island Helicopter, E 34th St Heliport ☎ 564-9290 (scheduled tours)

Liberty Helicopter, W 30th St Heliport ☎ 465-8905

New York Helicopter, E 34thSt Heliport ☎ 800/645-3494 (service to JFK)

Port Authority of NY and NJ, Downtown Manhattan Heliport ☎ 248-7240

Wall Street Helicopters, Downtown Manhattan Heliport ☎ 943-5959

TRAIN SERVICE

Amtrak, Grand Central Terminal, Park Ave & 42nd St ☎ 582-6875

Amtrak, Pennsylvania Station, Eighth Ave & 34th St ☎ 800/523-8720

Long Island Railroad (LIRR), Pennsylvania Station, Eighth Ave & 34th St ☎ 718/217-5477

Metro North, Grand Central Terminal, Park Ave & 42nd St ☎ 532-4900

New Jersey Transit, Pennsylvania Station, Eighth Ave & 34th St ☎ 800/626-7433 (NJ), 201/762-5100

PATH, Pennsylvania Station, Eighth Ave & 34th St ☎ 800/234-7284

BUS TERMINALS

George Washington Bridge Bus Station, Broadway & 178th St ☎ 564-1114

Port Authority Bus Terminal, Eighth Ave & 42nd St ☎ 564-8484

CRUISE TERMINALS

Passenger Ship Terminal, Piers 88-94 ☎ 246-5450

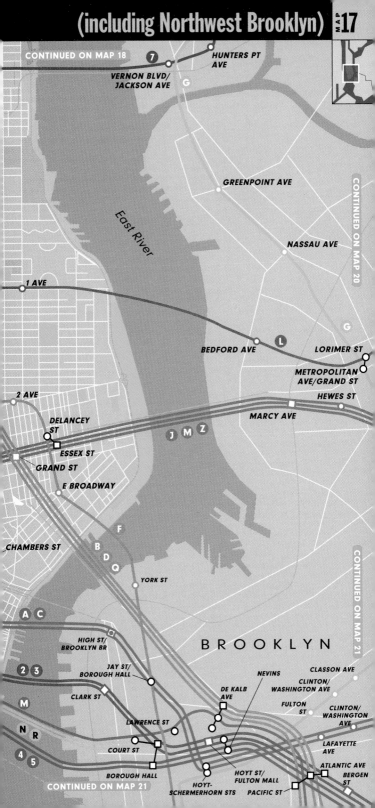

CONTINUED ON MAP 18

7

HUNTERS PT AVE

VERNON BLVD/ JACKSON AVE

G

CONTINUED ON MAP 20

GREENPOINT AVE

East River

NASSAU AVE

1 AVE

BEDFORD AVE

L

LORIMER ST

G

METROPOLITAN AVE/GRAND ST

2 AVE

HEWES ST

DELANCEY ST

MARCY AVE

ESSEX ST

J M Z

GRAND ST

E BROADWAY

F

CHAMBERS ST

B
D
Q

YORK ST

CONTINUED ON MAP 21

A C

BROOKLYN

HIGH ST/ BROOKLYN BR

2 3

JAY ST/ BOROUGH HALL

NEVINS

CLASSON AVE

CLINTON/ WASHINGTON AVE

M

CLARK ST

DE KALB AVE

FULTON ST

CLINTON/ WASHINGTON AVE

N R

LAWRENCE ST

4 5

COURT ST

LAFAYETTE AVE

BOROUGH HALL

HOYT ST/ FULTON MALL

ATLANTIC AVE

BERGEN ST

CONTINUED ON MAP 21

HOYT-SCHERMERHORN STS

PACIFIC ST

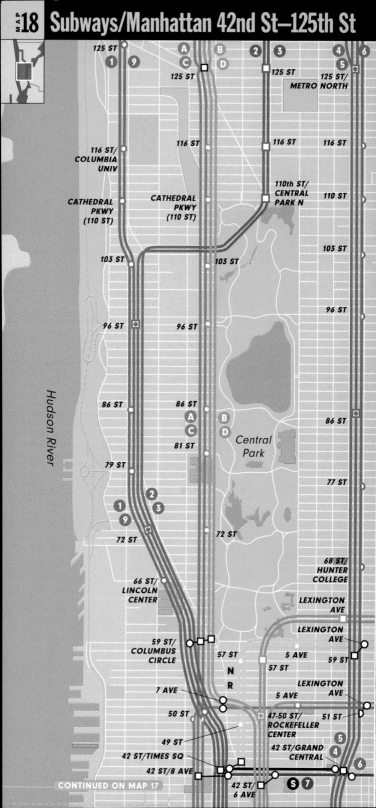

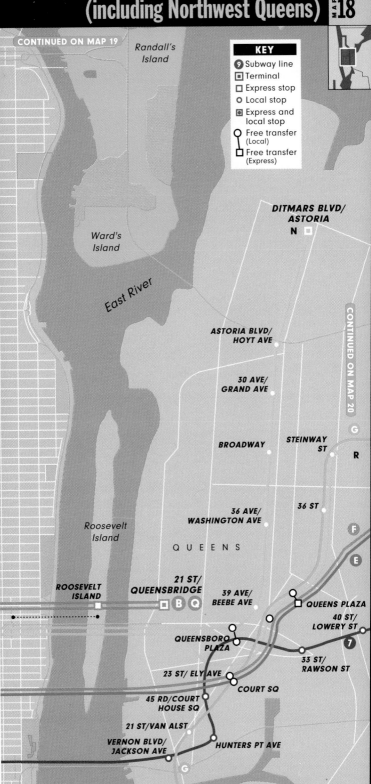

CONTINUED ON MAP 19

Randall's Island

KEY

● Subway line
▣ Terminal
☐ Express stop
○ Local stop
◉ Express and local stop
◯ Free transfer (Local)
☐ Free transfer (Express)

Ward's Island

DITMARS BLVD/ ASTORIA
N

East River

CONTINUED ON MAP 20

ASTORIA BLVD/ HOYT AVE

30 AVE/ GRAND AVE

G

BROADWAY
STEINWAY ST
R

36 ST

36 AVE/ WASHINGTON AVE

Roosevelt Island

F
E

Q U E E N S

21 ST/ QUEENSBRIDGE

39 AVE/ BEEBE AVE

ROOSEVELT ISLAND
B Q

QUEENS PLAZA

40 ST/ LOWERY ST

QUEENSBORO PLAZA

7

33 ST/ RAWSON ST

23 ST/ ELY AVE

COURT SQ

45 RD/COURT HOUSE SQ

21 ST/VAN ALST

VERNON BLVD/ JACKSON AVE
HUNTERS PT AVE

G

MAP 19 Subways/Bronx & Northern Manhattan

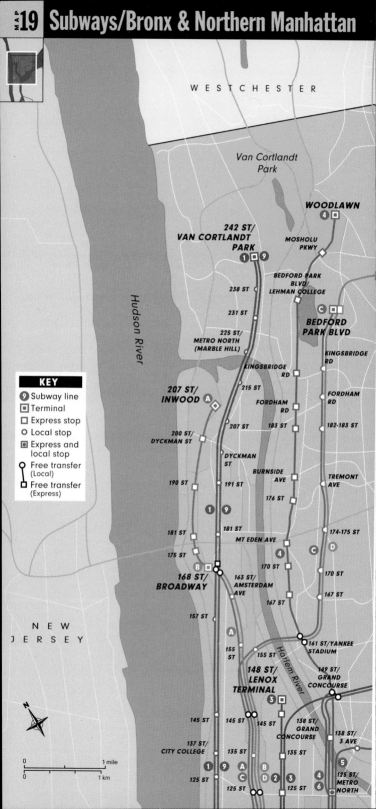

WESTCHESTER

Van Cortlandt
Park

WOODLAWN
4

MOSHOLU
PKWY

**242 ST/
VAN CORTLANDT
PARK**
1 9

BEDFORD PARK
BLVD/
LEHMAN COLLEGE

238 ST

231 ST

C

**BEDFORD
PARK BLVD**

225 ST/
METRO NORTH
(MARBLE HILL)

KINGSBRIDGE
RD

KINGSBRIDGE RD

Hudson River

215 ST

**207 ST/
INWOOD**
A

FORDHAM
RD

FORDHAM
RD

207 ST

183 ST

182-183 ST

200 ST/
DYCKMAN ST

DYCKMAN
ST

KEY
9 Subway line
Terminal
Express stop
Local stop
Express and
local stop
Free transfer
(Local)
Free transfer
(Express)

190 ST

191 ST

BURNSIDE
AVE

176 ST

TREMONT
AVE

1 9

181 ST

181 ST

MT EDEN AVE

174-175 ST

175 ST

4

C D

170 ST

170 ST

**168 ST/
BROADWAY**
B

163 ST/
AMSTERDAM
AVE

167 ST

167 ST

157 ST

NEW
JERSEY

A

155
ST

155 ST

161 ST/YANKEE
STADIUM

Harlem River

149 ST/
GRAND
CONCOURSE

**148 ST/
LENOX
TERMINAL**
3

N

138 ST/
GRAND
CONCOURSE

138 ST/
3 AVE

145 ST

145 ST

145 ST

5

137 ST/
CITY COLLEGE

135 ST

135 ST

125 ST/
METRO NORTH

0   1 mile
0   1 km

1 9 A
C

B
D 2

3

4
6

125 ST

125 ST

125 ST

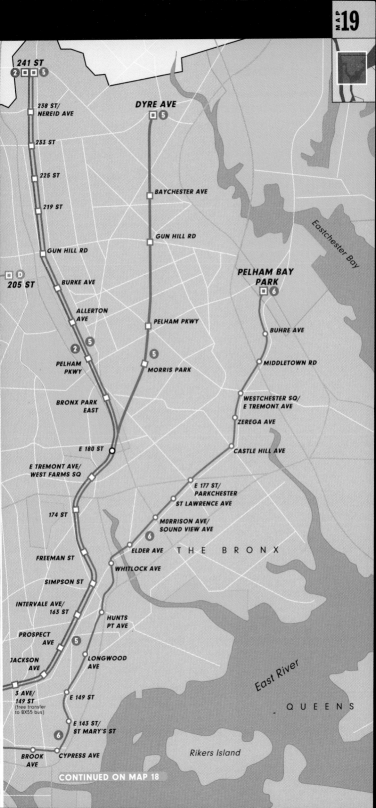

MAP 19

241 ST
2 □ □ □ 5

258 ST/
NEREID AVE

DYRE AVE
□ 5

233 ST

225 ST

BAYCHESTER AVE

219 ST

GUN HILL RD

GUN HILL RD

PELHAM BAY
PARK
□ 6

205 ST
D

BURKE AVE

BUHRE AVE

ALLERTON
AVE

PELHAM PKWY

MIDDLETOWN RD

2 5

PELHAM
PKWY

5

MORRIS PARK

WESTCHESTER SQ/
E TREMONT AVE

BRONX PARK
EAST

ZEREGA AVE

CASTLE HILL AVE

E 180 ST

E TREMONT AVE/
WEST FARMS SQ

E 177 ST/
PARKCHESTER

ST LAWRENCE AVE

174 ST

MORRISON AVE/
SOUND VIEW AVE

6

FREEMAN ST

ELDER AVE

T H E   B R O N X

WHITLOCK AVE

SIMPSON ST

INTERVALE AVE/
163 ST

HUNTS
PT AVE

PROSPECT
AVE

5

JACKSON
AVE

LONGWOOD
AVE

East River

3 AVE/
149 ST
(free transfer
to BX55 bus)

E 149 ST

Q U E E N S

E 143 ST/
ST MARY'S ST

6

BROOK
AVE

CYPRESS AVE

Rikers Island

Eastchester Bay

CONTINUED ON MAP 18

MAP 20 Subways/Queens & Northeast Brooklyn

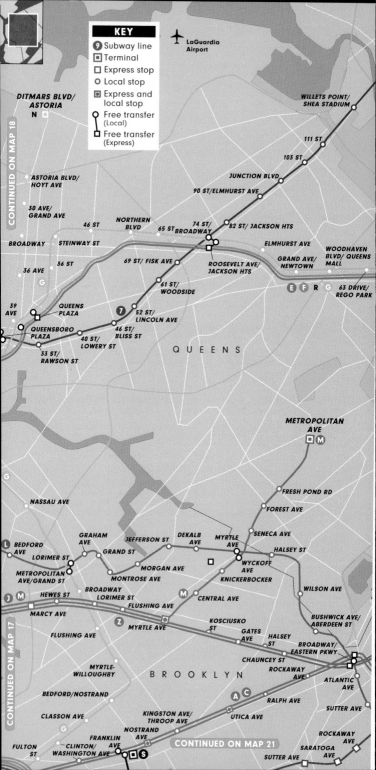

KEY
- **9** Subway line
- Terminal
- Express stop
- Local stop
- Express and local stop
- Free transfer (Local)
- Free transfer (Express)

LaGuardia Airport

CONTINUED ON MAP 18

DITMARS BLVD/ ASTORIA
N

WILLETS POINT/ SHEA STADIUM
111 ST
103 ST

ASTORIA BLVD/ HOYT AVE

JUNCTION BLVD
90 ST/ELMHURST AVE
82 ST/ JACKSON HTS

30 AVE/ GRAND AVE
46 ST
NORTHERN BLVD
65 ST/ BROADWAY
74 ST/ BROADWAY
ELMHURST AVE
WOODHAVEN BLVD/ QUEENS MALL

BROADWAY
STEINWAY ST
69 ST/ FISK AVE
ROOSEVELT AVE/ JACKSON HTS
GRAND AVE/ NEWTOWN

36 AVE
56 ST
E F R G
63 DRIVE/ REGO PARK

G
61 ST/ WOODSIDE

39 AVE
QUEENS PLAZA
52 ST/ LINCOLN AVE

QUEENSBORO PLAZA
40 ST/ LOWERY ST
46 ST/ BLISS ST
7

33 ST/ RAWSON ST

QUEENS

METROPOLITAN AVE
M

FRESH POND RD

FOREST AVE

NASSAU AVE

SENECA AVE

L
GRAHAM AVE
JEFFERSON ST
DEKALB AVE
MYRTLE AVE
HALSEY ST

BEDFORD AVE
LORIMER ST
GRAND ST
WYCKOFF AVE
WILSON AVE

METROPOLITAN AVE/GRAND ST
MORGAN AVE
MONTROSE AVE
KNICKERBOCKER

J M
HEWES ST
BROADWAY LORIMER ST
M
CENTRAL AVE
BUSHWICK AVE/ ABERDEEN ST

MARCY AVE
FLUSHING AVE
KOSCIUSKO ST
HALSEY ST
BROADWAY/ EASTERN PKWY

FLUSHING AVE
Z
MYRTLE AVE
GATES AVE
CHAUNCEY ST

MYRTLE- WILLOUGHBY
BROOKLYN
ROCKAWAY AVE
ATLANTIC AVE

BEDFORD/NOSTRAND
A C
RALPH AVE
SUTTER AVE

CLASSON AVE
KINGSTON AVE/ THROOP AVE
UTICA AVE

G
NOSTRAND AVE
ROCKAWAY AVE

FULTON ST
CLINTON/ WASHINGTON AVE
FRANKLIN AVE
S
CONTINUED ON MAP 21
SARATOGA AVE

SUTTER AVE

CONTINUED ON MAP 17

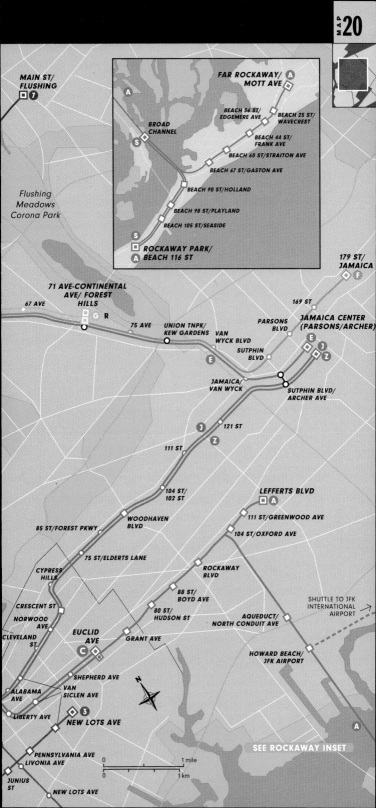

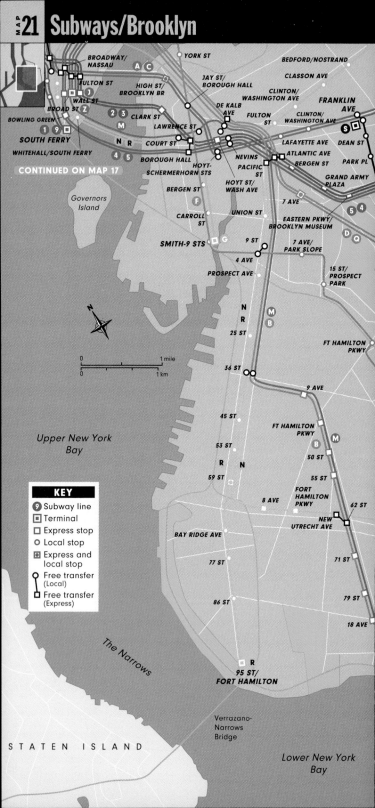

MAP 21 Subways/Brooklyn

BROADWAY/
NASSAU
YORK ST
BEDFORD/NOSTRAND
A C
CLASSON AVE
FULTON ST
JAY ST/
BOROUGH HALL
FRANKLIN
AVE
J
HIGH ST/
BROOKLYN BR
CLINTON/
WASHINGTON AVE
WALL ST
DE KALB
AVE
Z
2 3
CLARK ST
CLINTON/
WASHINGTON AVE
BROAD ST
BOWLING GREEN
FULTON
ST
S
1 9
M
LAWRENCE ST
LAFAYETTE AVE
DEAN ST
SOUTH FERRY
N R
COURT ST
ATLANTIC AVE
PARK PL
WHITEHALL/SOUTH FERRY
4 5
BERGEN ST
Borough Hall
NEVINS
ST
HOYT-
SCHERMERHORN STS
GRAND ARMY
PLAZA
CONTINUED ON MAP 17
PACIFIC
ST
BERGEN ST
HOYT ST/
WASH AVE
5 4
Governors
Island
F
7 AVE
CARROLL
ST
UNION ST
EASTERN PKWY/
BROOKLYN MUSEUM
D Q
SMITH-9 STS
G
9 ST
7 AVE/
PARK SLOPE
4 AVE
15 ST/
PROSPECT
PARK
PROSPECT AVE
N
R
25 ST
M
B
FT HAMILTON
PKWY
36 ST
9 AVE
Upper New York
Bay
45 ST
FT HAMILTON
PKWY
53 ST
M
B
50 ST
R
N
55 ST
59 ST
FORT
HAMILTON
PKWY
8 AVE
62 ST
NEW
UTRECHT AVE
BAY RIDGE AVE
71 ST

KEY
- **9** Subway line
- ▣ Terminal
- ▫ Express stop
- ○ Local stop
- ▣ Express and local stop
- ○—● Free transfer (Local)
- ▫—▪ Free transfer (Express)

77 ST
79 ST
86 ST
18 AVE

The Narrows

R
95 ST/
FORT HAMILTON

Verrazano-
Narrows
Bridge

STATEN ISLAND

Lower New York
Bay

MAP 21

CONTINUED ON MAP 20

Ⓐ Ⓒ
RALPH
AVE
UTICA AVE
SUTTER AVE/
RUTLAND RD
VAN SICLEN
AVE
PENNSYLVANIA
AVE
LIVONIA AVE
KINGSTON AVE/
THROOP AVE
NOSTRAND
AVE
JUNIUS ST
SUTTER AVE
ROCKAWAY
AVE
NEW LOTS AVE
KINGSTON
AVE
❸
SARATOGA
AVE
E 105 ST
NOSTRAND
AVE
UTICA AVE
❹
PRESIDENT ST
Ⓛ
ROCKAWAY
PKWY
FRANKLIN
AVE
STERLING ST
BOTANIC
GARDEN
WINTHROP ST
Ⓢ
PROSPECT
PARK
CHURCH AVE
PARKSIDE
AVE
BEVERLEY RD
CHURCH AVE
NEWKIRK AVE
BEVERLEY
RD
CORTELYOU
RD
❷ ❺
FLATBUSH AVE/
BROOKLYN
COLLEGE
CHURCH AVE
NEWKIRK AVE
B R O O K L Y N
DITMAS AVE
AVE H
18 AVE
AVE I
AVE J
18 AVE
20 AVE
Ⓓ
Ⓠ
BAY PKWY
Ⓕ
AVE M
AVE N
KINGS HWY
BAY PKWY
AVE P
18 AVE
20 AVE
KINGS HWY
KINGS HWY
AVE U
Ⓝ
AVE U
NECK RD
SHEEPSHEAD
BAY
Ⓜ BAY PKWY
AVE U
20 AVE
25 AVE
86 ST
AVE X
Ⓓ
NEPTUNE AVE/
VAN SICKLEN
BRIGHTON BEACH
BAY 50 ST
Ⓠ
OCEAN PKWY
Ⓝ
Ⓑ
W 8 ST/
AQUARIUM
Ⓕ Ⓓ
STILLWELL AVE/
CONEY ISLAND

Rockaway Inlet

MAP 22 Driving/Uptown Entrances & Exits

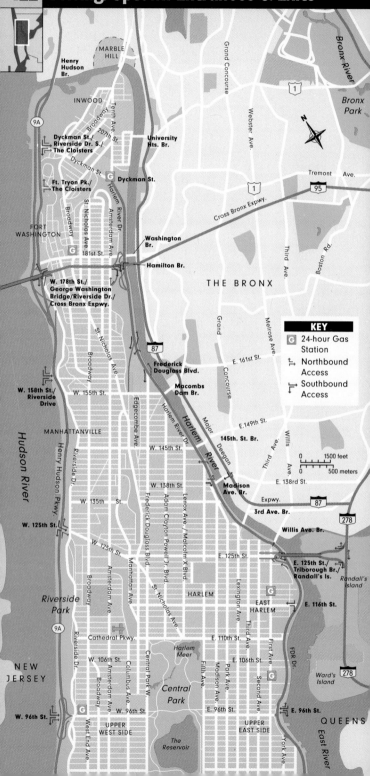

KEY

G 24-hour Gas Station

↰ Northbound Access

↱ Southbound Access

Henry Hudson Br.

MARBLE HILL

INWOOD

Dyckman St./ Riverside Dr. S./ The Cloisters

University Hts. Br.

G Dyckman St.

Ft. Tryon Pk./ The Cloisters

FORT WASHINGTON

G 181st St.

Washington Br.

Hamilton Br.

W. 178th St./ George Washington Bridge/Riverside Dr./ Cross Bronx Expwy.

Cross Bronx Expwy.

THE BRONX

Frederick Douglass Blvd.

Macombs Dam Br.

W. 158th St./ Riverside Drive

W. 155th St.

E. 161st St.

MANHATTANVILLE

W. 145th St.

145th St. Br.

E. 149th St.

W. 138th St.

Madison Ave. Br.

Major Deegan Expwy.

E. 138th St.

3rd Ave. Br.

W. 135th St.

W. 125th St.

W. 125th St.

Willis Ave. Br.

E. 125th St.

E. 125th St./ Triborough Br./ Randall's Is.

Randall's Island

HARLEM

EAST HARLEM

G

E. 116th St.

Riverside Park

Cathedral Pkwy.

Harlem Meer

E. 110th St.

W. 106th St.

E. 106th St.

G

NEW JERSEY

Central Park

Ward's Island

W. 96th St.

G W. 96th St.

UPPER WEST SIDE

The Reservoir

UPPER EAST SIDE

E. 96th St.

E. 96th St.

QUEENS

Hudson River

Riverside Park

East River

Bronx River

Bronx Park

Tremont Ave.

Grand Concourse

Webster Ave.

Third Ave.

Boston Rd.

Melrose Ave.

Willis Ave.

Lexington Ave.

First Ave.

Second Ave.

Fifth Ave.

Madison Ave.

Park Ave.

Third Ave.

York Ave.

FDR Dr.

Henry Hudson Pkwy.

Broadway

Amsterdam Ave.

St. Nicholas Ave.

Edgecombe Ave.

Manhattan Ave.

Adam Clayton Powell Jr. Blvd.

Frederick Douglass Blvd.

St. Nicholas Ave.

Lenox Ave./ Malcolm X Blvd.

Central Park W.

Columbus Ave.

Amsterdam Ave.

West End Ave.

Broadway

Riverside Dr.

Tenth Ave.

207th St.

Broadway

Dyckman St.

Harlem River Dr.

0   1500 feet

0   500 meters

Driving/Downtown Entrances & Exits

MAP 23

W. 96th St.
W. 92nd St.
W. 86th St.

E. 96th St.
E. 92nd St.
E. 92nd St.
E. 86th St.

The Reservoir

Central Park

W. 79th St. Boat Basin

W. 79th St.
W. 72nd St.
W. 72nd St.

The Lake

E. 79th St.
E. 79th St.

Roosevelt Island

E. 73rd St.
E. 72nd St.
E. 71st St.

UPPER WEST SIDE

UPPER EAST SIDE

E. 65th St.

W. 72nd St.

The Pond

E. 63rd St.
E. 61st St.

Central Park S.
E. 59th St.

LONG ISLAND CITY

Queensboro Bridge

W. 57th St.
W. 55th St.
W. 57th St.
W. 57th St.

QUEENS

W. 56th St.
W. 54th St.
W. 52nd St.
W. 51st St.
W. 50th St.
W. 49th St.
W. 50th St.

E. 53rd St.
E. 48th St.
E. 47th St.

W. 48th St.
W. 47th St.
W. 46th St.
W. 45th St.
W. 44th St.
W. 43rd St.
W. 42nd St.
W. 41st St.

MIDTOWN

THEATER DISTRICT

E. 42nd St.

Queens-Midtown Tunnel

GREENPOINT

495

W. 39 St./Javits Center

Lincoln Tunnel

MURRAY HILL

E. 37th St.

W. 34th St.
W. 34th St.
E. 34th St.
E. 34th St.

W. 30th St.
W. 29th St.

W. 26th St.

E. 25th St.
E. 23rd St.
E. 20th St.

W. 23rd St.
W. 23rd St.
CHELSEA

GRAMERCY

W. 18th St.

W. 14th St.
W. 14th St.
E. 14th St.
E. 14th St.

W. 12th St.

WEST VILLAGE

E. Houston St.

Hudson River

W. 12th St.
W. 11th St.

GREENWICH VILLAGE

EAST VILLAGE

NEW JERSEY

Christopher St.

NOHO
Houston St.

LOWER EAST SIDE

Clarkson St.
W. Houston St.

Delancey St.

Williamsburg Bridge

HOBOKEN

Holland Tunnel

SOHO

Bowery

Grand St.

DOWNTOWN

LITTLE ITALY

Cherry St.

Canal St.
Canal St.

Laight St.

TRIBECA

CHINATOWN

Manhattan Bridge

JERSEY CITY

West Side Hwy

Chambers St.

Civic Center

Flatbush Ave.

278

Barclay St.

Brooklyn Bridge

Vesey St.

BROOKLYN

FINANCIAL DISTRICT

SOUTH STREET SEAPORT

Liberty St.

BATTERY PARK CITY

BROOKLYN HEIGHTS

Morris St.

Whitehall

State St.

Battery Park

N

Brooklyn-Battery Tunnel

KEY

G 24-hour Gas Station

↥ Northbound Access

↧ Southbound Access

NOTE: West Side south of Chambers St. access on every street

0   1500 feet
0   500 meters

MAP 24 **Driving/Midtown Manhattan**

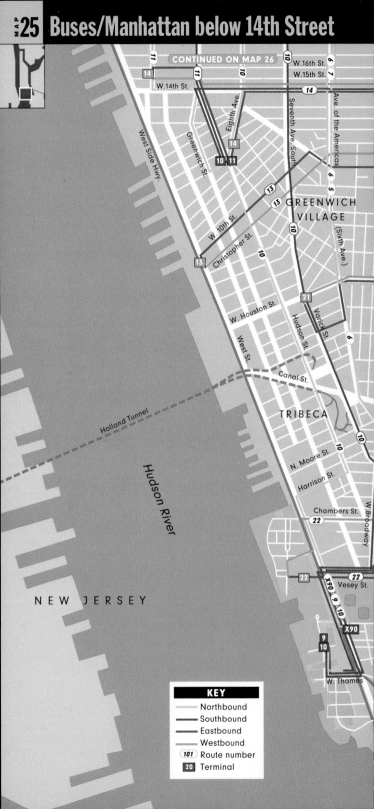

CONTINUED ON MAP 26

W.16th St.
W.15th St.
W.14th St.

Eighth Ave.

Greenwich St.

West Side Hwy.

Seventh Ave. South

Ave. of the Americas

GREENWICH
VILLAGE

(Sixth Ave.)

W. 10th St.

Christopher St.

Varick St.

W. Houston St.

West St.

Hudson St.

Canal St.

Holland Tunnel

TRIBECA

Hudson River

N. Moore St.

Harrison St.

Chambers St.

W. Broadway

NEW JERSEY

Vesey St.

Vesey St.

W. Thames

KEY

Northbound
Southbound
Eastbound
Westbound
(101) Route number
20 Terminal

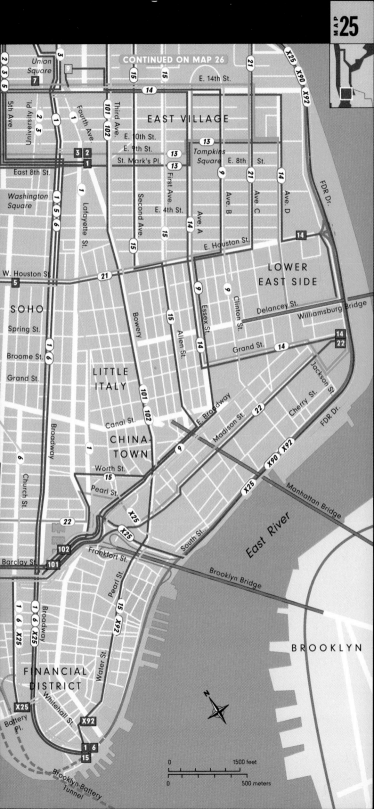

MAP 25

Union Square
② ③
② ③ ⑤
7

CONTINUED ON MAP 26

③

⑮
⑮

㉑

Ⓧ25 Ⓧ90 Ⓧ92

E. 14th St.

⑭

5th Ave.
University Pl.
Fourth Ave.
Third Ave.
① ①
101
102
② ③

EAST VILLAGE

E. 10th St.
E. 9th St.
St. Mark's Pl.
⑬
⑬
⑬
Tompkins Square
⑬
E. 8th St.
㉑
⑨
⑭

③ ②
①
East 8th St.

① ① ⑤ ⑥
①

First Ave.
Second Ave.

E. 4th St.
⑮
⑭
⑮

Ave. A
Ave. B
Ave. C
Ave. D
FDR Dr.

⑭

Washington Square

Lafayette St.

W. Houston St.
⑤
㉑

⑮

E. Houston St.

LOWER EAST SIDE

SOHO

Spring St.

① ⑥

Broome St.

Grand St.

⑥

Broadway

Church St.

LITTLE ITALY

Bowery

⑮

Allen St.

Essex St.
Clinton St.
⑨
⑨
⑨

Delancey St.

Williamsburg Bridge

⑭

Grand St.
⑭

⑭ ㉒

101
102

Canal St.

CHINA-TOWN

①

⑮

Worth St.

Pearl St.

㉒

Ⓧ25

102
101

Barclay St.

Frankfort St.

E. Broadway

Madison St.
㉒

⑨

Cherry St.

Jackson St.
FDR Dr.

Ⓧ90 Ⓧ92
Ⓧ25

South St.

Manhattan Bridge

East River

Brooklyn Bridge

BROOKLYN

① ⑥
① ⑥
Ⓧ25 Ⓧ25

Broadway

Pearl St.

Water St.

⑮
Ⓧ92

FINANCIAL DISTRICT

Ⓧ25

Whitehall St.
Ⓧ92

Battery Pl.

① ⑥
⑮

Brooklyn-Battery Tunnel

N

0   1500 feet
0   500 meters

MAP 26 **Buses/Manhattan 14th St–72nd St**

MAP 27
Buses/Manhattan 72nd St–125th St

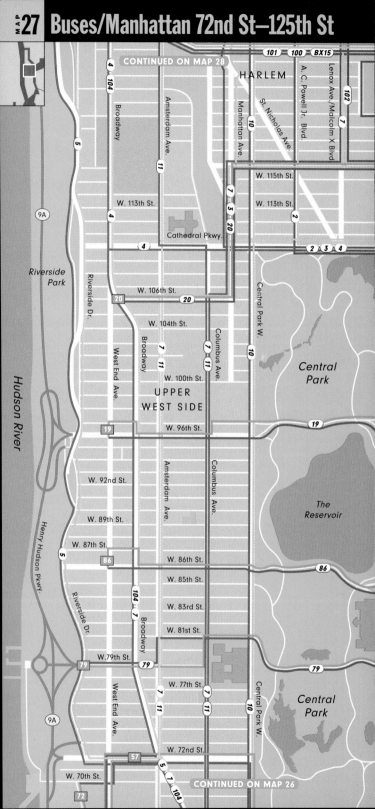

HARLEM

CONTINUED ON MAP 28

101 100 BX15
102

Broadway

Amsterdam Ave.

Manhattan Ave.

St. Nicholas Ave.

A. C. Powell Jr. Blvd.

Lenox Ave./Malcolm X Blvd

9A

Riverside Park

Riverside Dr.

Cathedral Pkwy.

W. 115th St.

W. 113th St.

W. 113th St.

Central Park W.

Central Park

The Reservoir

UPPER WEST SIDE

Hudson River

West End Ave.

Broadway

Amsterdam Ave.

Columbus Ave.

Henry Hudson Pkwy.

Riverside Dr.

W. 106th St.

W. 104th St.

W. 100th St.

W. 96th St.

W. 92nd St.

W. 89th St.

W. 87th St.

W. 86th St.

W. 85th St.

W. 83rd St.

W. 81st St.

W. 79th St.

W. 77th St.

W. 72nd St.

W. 70th St.

Central Park W.

Central Park

CONTINUED ON MAP 26

9A

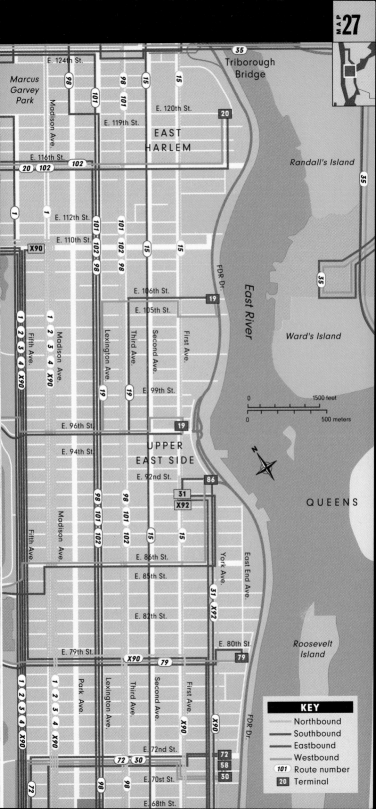

MAP 28 Buses/Manhattan above 125th Street

KEY
Northbound
Southbound
Eastbound
Westbound
101 Route number
20 Terminal

THE BRONX

MARBLE HILL

Inwood Hill Park

Fort Tryon Park

FORT WASHINGTON

WASHINGTON HEIGHTS

Hudson River

Harlem River

MANHATTANVILLE

HARLEM

EAST HARLEM

Cross Bronx Expwy.

Major Deegan Expwy.

Grand Concourse

Marcus Garvey Park

CONTINUED ON MAP 27

Top Attractions/Manhattan MAP 29

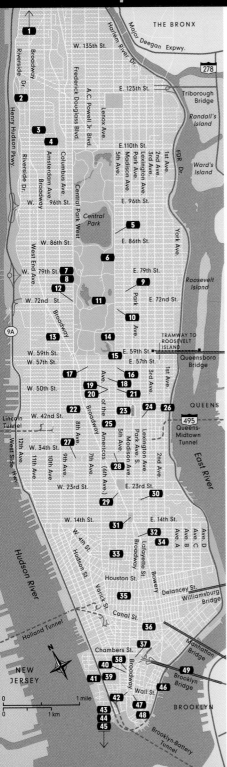

MAP **30** **Architecture**

MAP 30

Listed Alphabetically

MAP 31 **Churches & Temples**

MAP **31**

Listed by Site Number

1 Church of the Intercessions
2 Abyssinian Baptist
3 St Andrew's
4 Riverside
5 James Chapel
6 St Martin's Episcopal
7 St Paul's Chapel
8 Masjid Malcolm Shabazz
9 Cathedral of St John the Divine
10 NY Buddhist Church
11 Park Ave Synagogue
12 Park Ave Christian
13 St Ignatius Loyola
14 Church of the Holy Trinity
15 Holy Trinity
16 St Matthew & St Timothy
17 Congregation Rodeph Sholom
18 All Souls Unitarian
19 Church of St Jean Baptiste
20 Holy Trinity Cathedral
21 St James
22 West End Collegiate
23 Church of Latter Day Saints

24 Stephen Wise Free Synagogue
25 Fifth Ave Synagogue
26 Temple Emanu-El
27 St Vincent Ferrer
28 Christ Church
29 St Paul the Apostle
30 Calvary Baptist
31 Fifth Ave Presbyterian
32 Central Synagogue
33 St Peter's
34 St Thomas
35 St Patrick's Cathedral
36 St Bartholomew's
37 Holy Family
38 Church of the UN
39 Church of the Covenant
40 Church of Our Savior
41 Holy Apostles
42 Little Church Around the Corner
43 Marble Collegiate
44 Cathedral of St Sava
45 Friends Meeting House
46 Calvary/St George
47 Immaculate Conception

48 Church of the Ascension
49 Grace Church
50 St Mark's in the Bowery
51 St John's Evangelical Lutheran
52 Washington Square Church
53 Holy Trinity Chapel
54 Judson Memorial
55 Middle Collegiate
56 Church of St Luke's
57 St Peter's
58 St Paul's Chapel
59 John Street United Methodist
60 Trinity

Listed Alphabetically

Abyssinian Baptist, 2. 132 W 138th St ☎ 862-7474

All Souls Unitarian, 18. 1157 Lexington Ave ☎ 535-5530

Calvary Baptist, 30. 123 W 57th St ☎ 975-0170

Calvary/St George, 46. 209 E 16th St ☎ 475-0830. Episcopal

Cathedral of St John the Divine, 9. Amsterdam Ave & 112th St ☎ 316-7400. Episcopal

Cathedral of St Sava, 44. 15 W 25th St ☎ 242-9417. Serbian Orthodox

Central Synagogue, 32. 652 Lexington Ave ☎ 838-5122. Jewish

Christ Church, 28. 520 Park Ave ☎ 838-3036. Methodist

Church of the Ascension, 48. Fifth Ave & 10th St ☎ 254-8620. Episcopal

Church of the Covenant, 39. 310 E 42nd St ☎ 697-3185. Presbyterian

Church of the Holy Trinity, 14. 316 E 88th St ☎ 289-4100. Episcopal

Church of the Intercessions, 1. B'way & 155th St ☎ 283-6200. Episcopal

Church of Latter Day Saints, 23. 2 Lincoln Sq ☎ 580-1919. Mormon

Church of Our Savior, 40. 59 Park Ave ☎ 679-8166. Roman Catholic

Church of St Jean Baptiste, 19. 184 E 76th St ☎ 288-5082. Roman Catholic

Church of St Luke's, 56. 487 Hudson St ☎ 924-0562. Episcopal

Church of the UN, 38. 777 UN Plaza ☎ 661-1762. Inter-Denominational

Congregation Rodeph Sholom, 17. 7 W 83rd ☎ 362-8800. Jewish

Fifth Ave Presbyterian, 31. Fifth Ave & 55th St ☎ 247-0490

MAP 31 **Churches & Temples**

Listed Alphabetically (cont.)

Fifth Ave Synagogue, 25. 5 E 62nd St ☎ 838-2122. Jewish

Friends Meeting House, 45. 15 Rutherford Pl ☎ 777-8866. Quaker

Grace Church, 49. 802 Broadway ☎ 254-2000. Episcopal

Holy Apostles, 41. 296 Ninth Ave ☎ 807-6799. Episcopal

Holy Family, 37. 315 E 47th St ☎ 753-3401. Roman Catholic

Holy Trinity, 15. Central Park W & 65th St ☎ 877-6815. Lutheran

Holy Trinity Cathedral, 20. 319 E 74th St ☎ 288-3215. Greek Orthodox

Holy Trinity Chapel, 53. Washington Sq S ☎ 674-7236. Roman Catholic

Immaculate Conception, 47. 414 E 14th St ☎ 254-0200. Roman Catholic

James Chapel, 5. 3061 Broadway ☎ 280-1522. Inter-Denominational

John Street United Methodist, 59. 44 John St ☎ 269-0014

Judson Memorial, 54. 55 Washington Sq ☎ 477-0351. Baptist

Little Church Around the Corner, 42. 1 E 29th St ☎ 684-6770. Episcopal

Marble Collegiate, 43. Fifth Ave & 29th St ☎ 686-2770. Dutch Protestant

Masjid Malcolm Shabazz, 8. 102 W 116 St ☎ 662-2200. Muslim

Middle Collegiate, 55. Second Ave & 7th St ☎ 477-0666. Lutheran

NY Buddhist Church, 10. 332 Riverside Dr ☎ 678-0305

Park Ave Christian, 12. 1010 Park Ave ☎ 288-3246

Park Ave Synagogue, 11. 50 E 87th St ☎ 369-2600. Jewish

Riverside, 4. Riverside Dr & 122nd ☎ 222-5900. Inter-Denominational

St Andrew's, 3. Fifth Ave & 127th St ☎ 534-0896. Episcopal

St Bartholomew's, 36. 109 E 50th St ☎ 751-1616. Episcopal

St Ignatius Loyola, 13. 980 Park Ave ☎ 288-3588. Roman Catholic

St James, 21. 865 Madison Ave ☎ 288-4100. Episcopal

St John's Evangelical Lutheran, 51. 81 Christopher St ☎ 242-5737

St Mark's-in-the-Bowery, 50. Second Ave & 10th St ☎ 674-6377. Episcopal

St Martin's Episcopal, 6. 230 Lenox Ave ☎ 534-4531

St Matthew & St Timothy, 16. 26 W 84th St ☎ 362-6750. Episcopal

St Patrick's Cathedral, 35. Fifth Ave & 50th St ☎ 753-2261. Roman Catholic

St Paul the Apostle, 29. 415 W 59th St ☎ 265-3209. Roman Catholic

St Paul's Chapel, 58. Broadway & Fulton St ☎ 602-0874. Episcopal

St Paul's Chapel, 7. Columbia Univ, Broadway & 117th St ☎ 854-6625. Roman Catholic

St Peter's, 57. 16 Barclay St ☎ 233-8355. Roman Catholic

St Peter's, 33. 619 Lexington Ave ☎ 935-2200. Lutheran

St Thomas, 34. 1 W 53rd St ☎ 757-7013. Episcopal

St Vincent Ferrer, 27. Lexington Ave & 66th St ☎ 744-2080. Roman Catholic

Stephen Wise Free Synagogue, 24. 30 W 68th St ☎ 877-4050. Jewish

Temple Emanu-El, 26. 1 E 65th St ☎ 744-1400. Jewish

Trinity, 60. 74 Trinity Pl ☎ 602-0800. Episcopal

Washington Square Church, 52. 135 W 4th St ☎ 777-2528. Roman Catholic

West End Collegiate, 22. 245 W 77th St ☎ 787-1566. Reformed Church in America

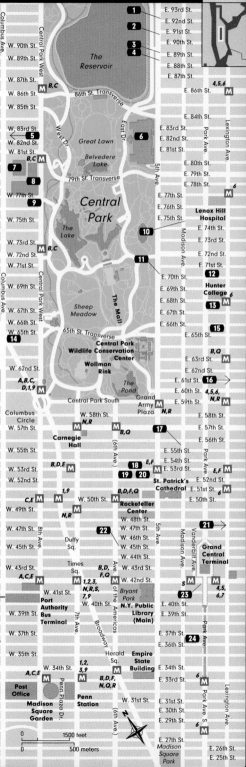

MAP 32 **Museums/Elsewhere in Manhattan**

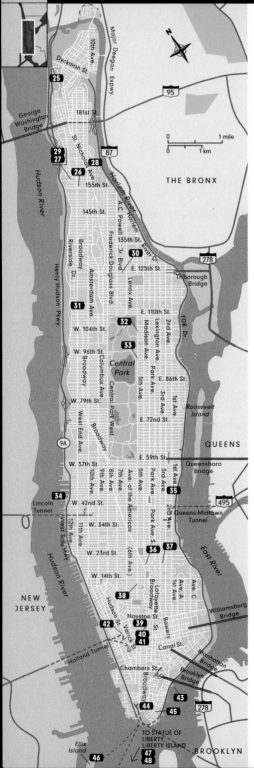

MAP **32**

Listed Alphabetically

Abigail Adams Smith, 16.
421 E 61st St ☎ 838-6878

African-American Institute, 35.
833 UN Plaza ☎ 949-5666

American Academy of Arts & Letters, 29. 633 W 155th St
☎ 368-5900

American Craft, 19. 40 W 53rd St
☎ 956-6047

American Museum of Immigration, 47.
Liberty Island ☎ 422-2150

American Museum of Natural History, 8. Central Park W & 79th St
☎ 769-5100

The Americas Society, 13.
680 Park Ave ☎ 249-8950

Asia Society Gallery, 12.
725 Park Ave ☎ 288-6400

Children's Museum of Manhattan, 5.
212 W 83rd St ☎ 721-1234

China Institute Gallery, 15.
125 E 65th St ☎ 744-8181

The Cloisters, 25. Fort Tryon Park
☎ 923-3700

Cooper-Hewitt/The Smithsonian, 2.
2 E 91st St ☎ 860-6898

Ellis Island Immigration, 46.
Ellis Island ☎ 363-7620

Forbes Magazine Galleries, 38.
62 Fifth Ave ☎ 206-5548

Fraunces Tavern, 45. 54 Pearl St
☎ 425-1778

Frick Collection, 11. 1 E 70th St
☎ 288-0700

Guggenheim, 4. 1071 Fifth Ave
☎ 423-3600

Guggenheim Soho, 40.
575 Broadway ☎ 423-3600

Hayden Planetarium, 7.
Central Park W & 80th St ☎ 769-5920

Hispanic Society of America, 27.
613 W 155th St ☎ 690-0743

Intrepid Sea-Air-Space, 34.
Pier 86, Twelfth Ave & W 46th St
☎ 245-0072

International Center of Photography, 33.
1130 Fifth Ave ☎ 860-1777

International Center of Photography/Midtown, 22. 1133 Ave of the Americas ☎ 768-4680

Japan Society, 21. 333 E 47th St
☎ 832-1155

Jewish, 1. 1109 Fifth Ave
☎ 423-3200

Metropolitan Museum of Art, 6. 1000 Fifth Ave ☎ 535-7710

Morris Jumel Mansion, 28.
1765 Jumel Ter ☎ 923-8008

Museum for African Art, 39.
593 Broadway ☎ 966-1313

Museum of American Folk Art, 14.
2 Lincoln Sq ☎ 595-9533

Museum of the American Indian, 44. 1 Bowling Green
☎ 668-6624

Museum of the City of NY, 32.
1220 Fifth Ave ☎ 534-1672

Museum of Modern Art (MOMA), 18. 11 W 53rd St ☎ 708-9480

Museum of Television & Radio, 20.
25 W 52nd St ☎ 621-6600

National Academy of Design, 3.
1083 Fifth Ave ☎ 369-4880

New Museum of Contemporary Art, 41. 583 Broadway ☎ 219-1222

NY Historical Society, 9.
170 Central Park W ☎ 873-3400

NYC Fire Museum, 42. 278 Spring St
☎ 691-1303

Nicholas Roerich, 31. 319 W 107th St
☎ 864-7752

Numismatic Society of America, 26.
Broadway & 155th St ☎ 234-3130

Pierpont Morgan Library, 24.
29 E 36th St ☎ 685-0610

Police Museum, 37. 235 E 20th St
☎ 477-9753

Sony Wonder Technology Lab, 17.
550 Madison Ave ☎ 833-5414

South Street Seaport, 43. Pier 17,
Fulton & South Sts ☎ 748-8600

Statue of Liberty Museum, 48.
Liberty Island ☎ 363-3200

Studio Museum in Harlem, 30.
144 W 125th St ☎ 864-4500

Theodore Roosevelt Birthplace, 36.
28 E 20th St ☎ 260-1616

Whitney Museum at Philip Morris, 23.
120 Park Ave ☎ 878-2453

Whitney Museum of American Art, 10.
945 Madison Ave ☎ 570-3676

MAP 33 Art Galleries/Uptown

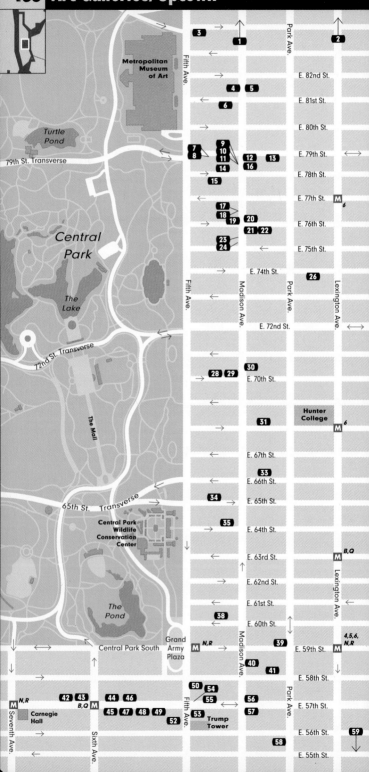

MAP 33

Listed by Site Number

E. 84th St.

E. 83rd St.

Third Ave.

Second Ave.

First Ave.

E. 73rd St.

E. 72nd St.

E. 71st St.

E. 70th St.

E. 69th St.

E. 68th St.

Third Ave.

Second Ave.

First Ave.

0   600 feet
0   200 meters

TRAMWAY TO ROOSEVELT ISLAND

Queensboro Bridge

Third Ave.

Second Ave.

First Ave.

25

27

32

36

37

Listed Alphabetically

Aberbach, 59. 675 Third Ave
☎ 988-1100

ACA, 56. 41 E 57th St
☎ 644-8300

Acquavella, 7. 18 E 79th St
☎ 734-6300

André Emmerich, 56. 41 E 57th St
☎ 752-0124

Arras, 53. 725 Fifth Ave ☎ 751-0080

Associated American Artists, 49.
20 W 57th St ☎ 399-5510

Barbara Mathes, 56. 41 E 57th St
☎ 752-5135

Blum Helman, 49. 20 W 57th St
☎ 245-2888

Brewster, 44. 41 W 57th St
☎ 980-1975

CDS, 13. 76 E 79th St ☎ 772-9555

Christie's, 39. 502 Park Ave
☎ 546-1000

Christie's East, 32. 219 E 67th St
☎ 606-0400

Cordier & Ekstrom, 25. 417 E 75th St
☎ 988-8857

David Findlay, 18. 984 Madison Ave
☎ 249-2909

David Findlay Jr, 56. 41 E 57th St
☎ 486-7660

Davis & Langdale Co, 37. 231 E 60th
St ☎ 838-0333

Davlyn, 20. 975 Madison Ave
☎ 879-2075

De Rempich, 30. 851 Madison Ave
☎ 772-6855

Elkon, 6. 18 E 81st St ☎ 535-3940

Fischbach, 48. 24 W 57th St
☎ 759-2345

Fitch & Febvrel, 54. 5 E 57th St
☎ 688-8522

Forum, 50. 745 Fifth Ave ☎ 355-4545

Frumkin & Adams, 45. 50 W 57th St
☎ 757-6655

Galerie Lelong, 49. 20 W 57th St
☎ 315-0470

Galerie Naive, 2. 145 E 92nd St
☎ 427-9283

Galerie St Etienne, 48. 24 W 57th St
☎ 245-6734

Grace Borgenicht, 52. 724 Fifth Ave
☎ 247-2111

Graham, 9. 1014 Madison Ave
☎ 535-5767

H.V. Allison, 33. 47 E 66th St
☎ 472-1455

Hammer, 46. 33 W 57th St
☎ 644-4400

Hirschl & Adler, 28. 21 E 70th St
☎ 535-8810

Isselbacher, 14. 41 E 78th St
☎ 472-1766

James Goodman, 56. 41 E 57th St
☎ 593-3737

Jan Krugier, 56. 41 E 57th St
☎ 755-7288

Jordan-Volpe, 23. 958 Madison Ave
☎ 570-9500

Kennedy, 51. 730 Fifth Ave
☎ 541-9600

Kenneth Lux, 30. 851 Madison Ave
☎ 861-6839

Knoedler, 29. 19 E 70th St
☎ 794-0550

Kraushaar, 52. 724 Fifth Ave
☎ 307-5730

Leloup, 4. 1080 Madison Ave
☎ 772-3410

Littlejohn-Contemporary, 56.
41 E 57th St ☎ 980-2323

Marion Goodman, 48. 24 W 57th St
☎ 977-7160

Marisa Del Re, 56. 41 E 57th St
☎ 688-1843

Marlborough, 47. 40 W 57th St
☎ 541-4900

Martin Sumers, 45. 50 W 57th St
☎ 541-8334

McCoy, 56. 41 E 57th St ☎ 319-1996

McKee, 50. 745 Fifth Ave ☎ 688-5951

Midtown Payson, 50. 745 Fifth Ave
☎ 758-1900

Multiples, 48. 24 W 57th St
☎ 977-7160

Pace Editions, 57. 32 E 57th St
☎ 421-3292

Paolo Baldacci, 56. 41 E 57th St
☎ 826-4210

Paul Drey, 55. 11 E 57th St
☎ 753-2551

Perls, 10. 1016 Madison Ave
☎ 472-3200

Peter Findlay, 56. 41 E 57th St
☎ 644-4433

Raydon, 5. 1091 Madison Ave
☎ 288-3555

MAP 33

Listed Alphabetically (cont.)

Reece, 48. 24 W 57th St ☎ 333-5830

Richard L. Feigen, 31. 49 E 68th St
☎ 628-0700

Richard York, 34. 21 E 65th St
☎ 772-9155

Robert Mann, 22. 42 E 76th St
☎ 570-1223

Robert Miller, 56. 41 E 57th St
☎ 980-5454

Ronin, 40. 605 Madison Ave
☎ 688-0188

Rosenberg & Steibel, 57. 32 E 57th St
☎ 753-4368

Safani, 19. 980 Madison Ave
☎ 570-6360

Saidenberg, 11. 1018 Madison Ave
☎ 288-3387

Salander-O'Reilly, 8. 20 E 79th St
☎ 879-6606

Schweitzer, 3. 18 E 84th St
☎ 535-5430

Sid Deutsch, 36. 305 E 61st St
☎ 754-6660

Sidney Janis, 42. 110 W 57th St
☎ 586-0110

Sindin, 24. 956 Madison Ave
☎ 288-7902

Solomon & Co, 21. 959 Madison Ave
☎ 737-8200

Sotheby's, 27. 1334 York Ave
☎ 606-7000

Soufer, 16. 1015 Madison Ave
☎ 628-3225

Spanierman, 41. 45 E 58th St
☎ 832-0208

Sportsman's Edge, 26. 136 E 74th St
☎ 249-5010

Stiebel Modern, 57. 32 E 57th St
☎ 759-5536

Studio 53, 58. 424 Park Ave
☎ 755-6650

Suzuki, 48. 24 W 57th St
☎ 582-0373

Sylvan Cole, 43. 101 W 57th St
☎ 333-7760

Tatistcheff & Co, 45. 50 W 57th St
☎ 664-0907

Terry Dintenfass, 12. 20 E 79th St
☎ 581-2268

Tibor de Nagy, 44. 41 W 57th St
☎ 421-3780

Ubu, 15. 16 E 78th St
☎ 794-4444

The Uptown, 1. 1194 Madison
Ave ☎ 722-3677

Viridian, 48. 24 W 57th St
☎ 245-2882

Wally Findlay, 38. 14 E 60th St
☎ 421-5390

Washburn, 49. 20 W 57th St
☎ 397-6780

Weintraub, 17. 988 Madison
☎ 879-1132

Wildenstein, 35. 19 E 64th St
☎ 879-0500

Zabriskie, 52. 724 Fifth Ave
☎ 307-7430

MAP 34   Art Galleries/SoHo

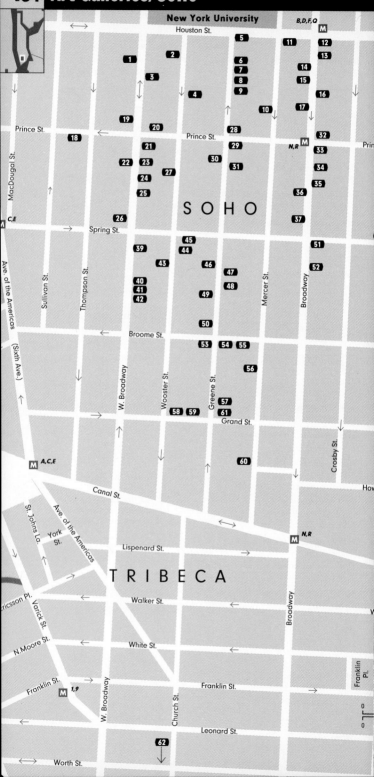

MAP 34

Listed by Site Number

MAP 34 Art Galleries/SoHo

Listed Alphabetically

Amos Eno, 12. 594 Broadway
☎ 226-5342

Anne Phenab, 46. 81 Greene St
☎ 219-2007

Artists Space, 61. 38 Greene St
☎ 226-3970

Atlantic, 53. 475 Broome St
☎ 219-3183.

Barbara Gladstone, 30.
99 Greene St ☎ 431-3334

Bess Cutler, 42. 379 W Broadway
☎ 219-1577

Blum Helman Warehouse, 47.
80 Greene St ☎ 226-8770

Brooke Alexander, 43.
59 Wooster St ☎ 925-4338

Bruce R Lewin, 21. 136 Prince St
☎ 431-4750

Charles Cowles, 22.
420 W Broadway ☎ 925-3500

Condeso/Lawler, 51. 524 Broadway
☎ 219-1283

Curt Marcus, 16. 578 Broadway
☎ 226-3200

Dia Center for the Arts, 39.
393 W Broadway ☎ 925-9397

DCA, 22. 420 W Broadway
☎ 334-3331

Dyansen of Soho, 1.
462 W Broadway ☎ 982-3668

Edward Thorp, 28. 103 Prince St
☎ 431-6880

EM Donahue, 33. 560 Broadway
☎ 226-1111

Exit Art, 35. 548 Broadway
☎ 966-7745

Fawbush, 59. 76 Grand St
☎ 274-0660

Feature, 48. 76 Greene St
☎ 941-7077

55 Mercer, 56. 55 Mercer St
☎ 226-8513

First St, 33. 560 Broadway
☎ 226-9127

Franklin Parrasch, 13. 588 Broadway
☎ 925-7090

Gagosian, 4. 136 Wooster St
☎ 228-2878

Gallery Henoch, 44. 80 Wooster St
☎ 966-0303

Harvey, 36. 537 Broadway
☎ 925-7651

Heller, 49. 71 Greene St ☎ 966-5948

Holly Solomon, 11. 172 Mercer
☎ 941-5777

Interart Center, 26. 167 Spring St
☎ 431-7500

Jay Gorney, 31. 100 Greene St
☎ 966-4480

John Gibson, 32. 568 Broadway
☎ 925-1192

June Kelly, 14. 591 Broadway
☎ 226-1660

Klarfeld Perry, 50. 472 Broome St
☎ 941-0303

Leo Castelli, 22. 420 W Broadway
☎ 431-5160

Leo Castelli (2), 16. 578 Broadway
☎ 431-6279

Mary Boone, 24. 417 W Broadway
☎ 431-1818

Max Protech, 33. 560 Broadway
☎ 966-5454

Meisel, 20. 141 Prince St ☎ 677-1340

Metro Pictures, 5. 150 Greene St
☎ 925-8335

Nahan Contemporary, 41.
381 W Broadway ☎ 966-9313

Nancy Hoffman, 23.
429 W Broadway ☎ 966-6676

**New Museum of Contemporary Art,
15.** 583 Broadway ☎ 219-1355

Nosei, 29. 100 Prince St ☎ 431-9253

OK Harris, 40. 383 W Broadway
☎ 431-3600

Pace, 6. 142 Greene St ☎ 431-9224

Pamela Auchincloss, 34.
558 Broadway ☎ 966-7753

Paul Kasmin, 58. 74 Grand St
☎ 219-3219

Paula Cooper, 2. 155 Wooster St
☎ 674-0766

Penine Hart, 55. 457 Broome St
☎ 226-2761

Phoenix, 32. 568 Broadway
☎ 226-8711

Phyllis Kind, 8. 136 Greene St
☎ 925-1200

Postmasters, 47. 80 Greene St
☎ 941-5711

PPOW, 37. 532 Broadway
☎ 941-8642

Ronald Feldman, 60. 31 Mercer St
☎ 226-3232

MAP **34**

Listed Alphabetically (cont.)

Reusch, 45. 134 Spring St
☎ 925-1137

Sally Hawkins, 19. 448 W Broadway
☎ 477-5699

Sigma, 40. 379 W Broadway
☎ 941-0014

SoHo 20, 54. 469 Broome St
☎ 226-4167

Solo Impression, 52. 520 Broadway
☎ 925-3599

Sonnabend, 22. 420 W Broadway
☎ 966-6160

Sperone Westwater, 7.
142 Greene St ☎ 431-3685

Sragow, 38. 73 Spring St ☎ 219-1793

Stark, 33. 560 Broadway
☎ 925-4484

Steinbaum Krauss, 9. 132 Greene St
☎ 431-4224

Stephen Haller, 33. 560 Broadway
☎ 219-2500

Stux, 10. 163 Mercer St ☎ 219-0010

Susan Teller, 32. 568 Broadway
☎ 941-7335

Tenri, 17. 575 Broadway ☎ 925-8500

Tony Shafrazi, 27. 119 Wooster St
☎ 274-9300

Vorpal, 3. 459 W Broadway
☎ 334-3939

Ward-Nasse, 18. 178 Prince St
☎ 925-6951

Wessel O'Connor, 62.
60 Thomas St ☎ 406-0040

Witkin, 25. 415 W Broadway
☎ 925-5510

Zarre, 57. 48 Greene St ☎ 966-2222

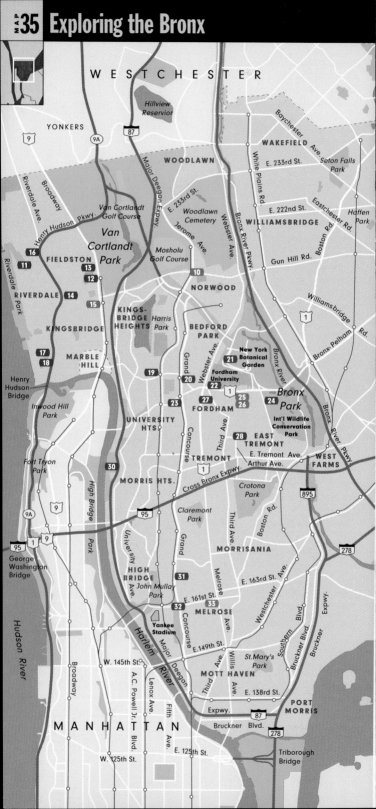

MAP 35 **Exploring the Bronx**

WESTCHESTER

Hillview
Reservoir

YONKERS

9

9A

87

WOODLAWN

Van Cortlandt
Golf Course

E. 233rd St.

Woodlawn
Cemetery

Jerome Ave.

Webster Ave.

Bronx River Pkwy.

White Plains Rd.

WAKEFIELD

E. 233rd St.

Seton Falls
Park

E. 222nd St.

Eastchester Rd

Haffen
Park

WILLIAMSBRIDGE

Boston Rd.

Gun Hill Rd.

Williamsbridge
Rd.

1

Bronx Pelham

Riverdale Ave.

Broadway

Henry Hudson Pkwy.

**Van
Cortlandt
Park**

16

11

FIELDSTON

13

12

RIVERDALE

14

15

Riverdale
Park

KINGSBRIDGE

KINGS-
BRIDGE
HEIGHTS

Harris
Park

Mosholu
Golf Course

10

NORWOOD

Grand Ave.

BEDFORD
PARK

Webster Ave.

21

New York
Botanical
Garden

Fordham
University

22

**Bronx
Park**

17

18

Henry
Hudson
Bridge

MARBLE
HILL

19

20

23

27

FORDHAM

25
26

24

Int'l Wildlife
Conservation
Park

Bronx River

Bronx River Pkwy.

Inwood Hill
Park

Fort Tryon
Park

High Bridge Park

UNIVERSITY
HTS.

Concourse

28

EAST
TREMONT

E. Tremont Ave.

Arthur Ave.

WEST
FARMS

30

TREMONT

1

9A

9

MORRIS HTS.

Cross Bronx Expwy.

95

Claremont
Park

Crotona
Park

Third Ave.

Boston Rd.

895

278

95

1

9

George
Washington
Bridge

University Ave.

Grand Ave.

HIGH
BRIDGE

John Mullay
Park

31

Melrose Ave.

MORRISANIA

Third Ave.

E. 163rd St.

Westchester Ave.

Southern Blvd.

Bruckner Blvd.

Bruckner Expwy.

Hudson River

Broadway

W. 145th St.

A.C. Powell Jr. Blvd.

Lenox Ave.

Fifth Ave.

Harlem River

Major Deegan

32

E. 161st St.

MELROSE

Concourse

**Yankee
Stadium**

E.149th St.

Third Ave.

Willis Ave.

St. Mary's
Park

33

MOTT HAVEN

E. 138th St.

PORT
MORRIS

MANHATTAN

W. 125th St.

E. 125th St.

Expwy.

Bruckner Blvd.

87

278

Triborough
Bridge

MAP **35**

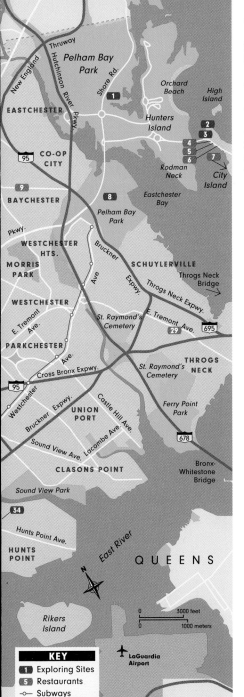

Bronx Listed by Site Number

MAP 36 **Exploring Brooklyn**

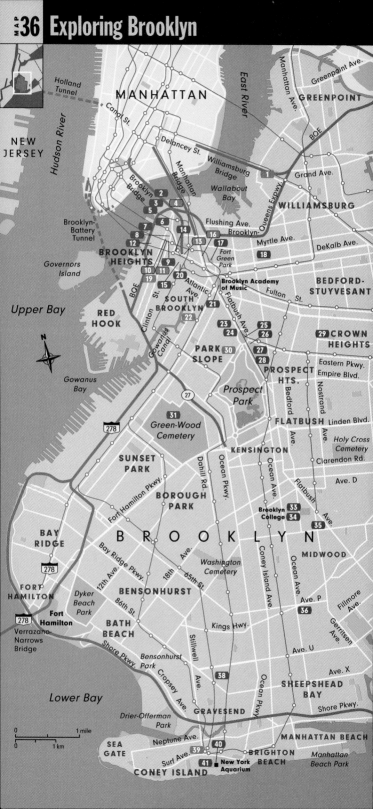

MAP **36**

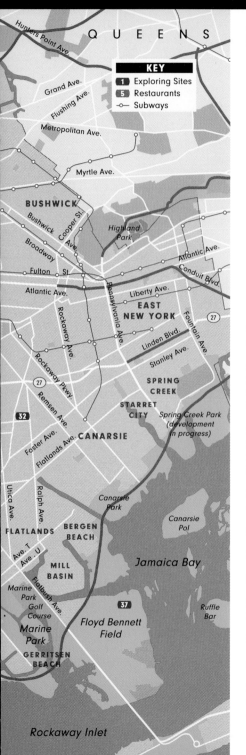

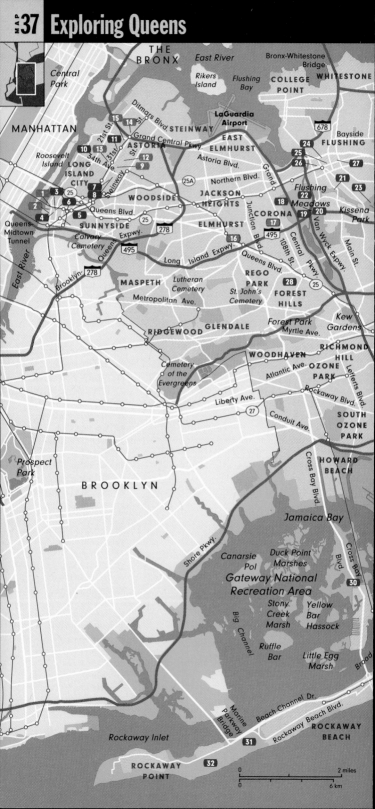

MAP 37

Queens Listed by Site Number

1. Water's Edge Restaurant
2. Café Vernon
3. Silvercup Studios
4. PS 1 Museum
5. International Design Center
6. Court House Square
7. American Museum of the Moving Image
8. Kaufman Astoria Studios
9. Karyatis
10. Isamu Noguchi Garden Museum
11. St Demitrios
12. Zenon Taverna Meze House
13. Roumeli Taverna
14. Elias Corner
15. Piccola Venezia
16. Jai Ya Thai
17. Park Side
18. NY Hall of Science
19. World's Fair Ice Skating Rink
20. Queens Museum
21. Queens Botanical Gardens
22. Flushing Meadows-Corona Park
23. Kissena Park
24. Friends Meeting House
25. Bowne House
26. Queens Historical Society
27. Weeping Beech Tree
28. West Side Tennis Club
29. St John's Univ
30. Jamaica Bay Wildlife Refuge
31. Jacob Riis Park
32. Fort Tilden

MAP 38 Exploring Staten Island

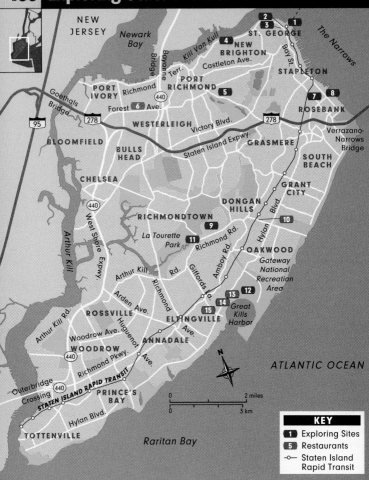

KEY
1 Exploring Sites
5 Restaurants
○—○ Staten Island Rapid Transit

Staten Island Listed by Site Number

1 Staten Island Ferry
2 Museum of Staten Island
3 Staten Island Institute
4 Snug Harbor Cultural Center
5 Staten Island Zoo
6 Real Madrid
7 Garibaldi-Meucci Museum
8 Alice Austin House
9 Jaques Marchais Center of Tibetan Art
10 Pennyfeathers

11 Richmondtown Restoration, Staten Island Historical Society
12 Gateway National Recreation Area
13 Windjammer
14 Marina Cafe
15 Arirang

MAP 35

Outer Boroughs Listed Alphabetically

BRONX SITES

Arthur Ave Italian Market, 28. Arthur Ave, betw E Fordham Rd & E Tremont Ave

Bartow-Pell Mansion, 1. Shore Rd & Pelham Bay Pkwy ☏ 718/885-1461

Bronx County Courthouse, 32. 851 Grand Concourse ☏ 718/590-3646

Bronx Museum of the Arts, 31. 1040 Grand Concourse ☏ 718/681-6000

Bronx Zoo (IWCP), 24. Fordham Rd & Southern Blvd ☏ 718/367-1010

Christ Church, 16. Henry Hudson Pkwy & 252nd St

City Island, 2. Long Island Sound

Creston Ave Baptist Church, 23. 114 E 188th St ☏ 718/367-1754

Edgar Allan Poe Cottage, 20. Grand Concourse & E Kingsbridge Rd ☏ 718/881-8900

Edgehill Church, 18. 2570 Independence Ave ☏ 718/549-7324

Enrico Fermi Cultural Center/Library, 27. 610 E 186th St ☏ 718/933-6410

Fordham University, 22. 441 E Fordham Rd ☏ 718/817-1000

Henry Hudson Memorial, 17. Independence Ave & W 227th St

Hunts Point Market & Sculpture Park, 34. Hunts Pt Ave & Food Ctr Dr ☏ 718/931-9500

Kingsbridge Armory, 19. Kingsbridge Rd & Jerome Ave ☏ 718/367-4350

Manhattan College, 13. Manhattan Col Pkwy & W 242nd St ☏ 718/920-0100

North Wind Undersea Museum, 3. 610 City Island Ave ☏ 718/885-0701

NY Botanical Garden, 21. Southern Blvd & 200th St ☏ 718/817-8500

Pelham Bay Park, 8. Pelham Bay

Roberto Clemente State Park, 30. W Tremont Ave & Matthewson Rd ☏ 718/299-8750

Van Cortlandt House Museum, 12. B'way & W 246th St ☏ 718/543-3344

Wave Hill, 11. 675 W 252nd St ☏ 718/549-3200

World War I Memorial Tower, 14. Riverdale Ave & 239th St

BRONX RESTAURANTS

Alex & Henry's Restaurant, 33. 862 Cortlandt Ave ☏ 718/585-3290. Italian. $

Amerigo's, 29. 3587 E Tremont Ave ☏ 718/792-3600. Italian. $$

Amici's Italian Restaurant, 4. 566 E 187th St ☏ 718/364-8598. Italian. $$

Ann & Tony's Restaurant, 25. 2407 Arthur Ave ☏ 718/364-8250. Italian. $$

Dominick's, 26. 2335 Arthur Ave ☏ 718/733-2807. Italian. $$

Il Boschetto Finest Italian, 9. 1660 E Gunn Hill Rd ☏ 718/379-9335. Italian. $$$

King Lobster, 6. 500 City Island Ave ☏ 718/885-1579. Seafood. $$

Portofino Restaurant, 5. 555 City Island Ave ☏ 718/885-1220. Continental. $$$

Riverdale Diner, 15. 3657 Kingsbridge Ave ☏ 718/884-6050. Diner. $

Sammy's Fish Box, 7. 41 City Island Ave ☏ 718/885-0920. Seafood. $$$

Sincere Garden, 10. 89 E Gunhill Rd ☏ 718/882-5923. Chinese. $$

MAP 36

BROOKLYN SITES

Bargemusic, Ltd, 5. Fulton Ferry Landing, Old Fulton St & Waterfront ☏ 718/624-4061

Bklyn Acad of Music (BAM), 21. 30 Lafayette Ave ☏ 718/636-4100

Bklyn Borough Hall, 14. 209 Joralemon St

Bklyn Botanic Garden, 28. 1000 Washington Ave ☏ 718/622-4433

Bklyn Bridge, 2. Parkes Cadman Plaza, Bklyn, to City Hall Park, Manhattan

Bklyn Center of Performing Arts, 34. Brooklyn College, Bedford & H Aves ☏ 718/951-4500

Bklyn Children's Museum, 29. 145 Brooklyn Ave ☏ 718/735-4432

Bklyn College CUNY, 33. Bedford & H Aves ☏ 718/951-5000

$$$$ = *over $50* $$$ = *$30-$50* $$ = *$20-$30* $ = *under $20*
Based on cost per person, excluding drinks, service, and 8 1/4% sales tax.

MAP 36

Outer Boroughs Listed Alphabetically (Cont.)

BROOKLYN SITES (cont.)

Bklyn Conservatory of Music, 23. 58 7th Ave ☎ 718/622-3300

Brooklyn Historical Society, 8. 128 Pierrepont St ☎ 718/624-0890

Brooklyn Museum, 27. 200 Eastern Pkwy ☎ 718/638-5000

Brooklyn Public Library, 26. Flatbush Ave & Eastern Pkwy ☎ 718/780-7700

Church of St Ann & the Holy Trinity, 9. 157 Montague St ☎ 718/834-8794

Coe House, 35. 1128 E 34th St

Coney Island Amusement Park, 41. Surf Ave ☎ 718/372-0275

Fulton Ferry Pier, 3. foot of Old Fulton St

Gateway National Recreation Area, 37. Floyd Bennet Field, Flatbush Ave & Shore Pkwy ☎ 718/338-3338

Green-Wood Cemetery, 31. Fifth Ave & 25th St ☎ 718/768-7300

Long Island Univ, 17. Univ Plaza, DeKalb & Flatbush Aves ☎ 718/488-1000

Montauk Club, 24. 25 Eighth Ave ☎ 718/638-0800

NY Aquarium, 40. Boardwalk & W 8th St ☎ 718/265-3475

NY Transit Museum, 15. Boerum Pl & Schermerhorn St ☎ 718/330-3060

Old Gravesend Cemetery, 38. Gravesend Neck Rd & MacDonald Ave

Our Lady of Lebanon Roman Catholic Church, 12. 113 Remsen St ☎ 718/624-7228

Plymouth Church, 6. 75 Hicks St

☎ 718/624-4743

Pratt Institute, 18. 200 Willoughby Ave ☎ 718/636-3600

The Promenade, 7. Atlantic, Montague & Clark Sts

Soldiers' & Sailors' Memorial Arch, 25. Grand Army Plaza, Flatbush Ave & Eastern Pkwy

State St Houses, 20. 290-324 State St

Wyckoff House/Pieter Claesen, 32. 5816 Clarendon Rd ☎ 718/629-5400

Wyckoff-Bennett Homestead, 36. 1669 E 22nd St

BROOKLYN RESTAURANTS

Cammareri Brothers Bakery, 19. 502 Henry St ☎ 718/852-3606. Bakery. $

Gage & Tollner, 13. 372 Fulton St ☎ 718/875-5181. American. $$$

Garginlo's Restaurant, 39. 2911 W 15th St ☎ 718/266-4891. Italian. $$

Junior's Restaurant, 16. 386 Flatbush Ave ☎ 718/852-5257. American. $

Leaf & Bean of Bklyn Hts, 11. 136 Montague St ☎ 718/638-5791. Polish. $

Monte's, 22. 451 Carroll St ☎ 718/624-8984. Italian. $$

Peter Luger Steak House, 1. 178 B'way ☎ 718/387-7400. Steakhouse. $$$$

River Cafe, 4. 1 Water St ☎ 718/522-5200. Continental. $$$$

Teresa's, 10. 80 Montague St ☎ 718/797-3996. Polish. $

Two Boots Restaurant, 30. 514 2nd St ☎ 718/499-3253. Italian. $

MAP 37

QUEENS SITES

American Museum of the Moving Image, 7. 35th Ave & 36th St ☎ 718/784-0077

Bowne House, 25. 37-01 Bowne St ☎ 718/359-0528

Court House Square, 6. 45th Ave & 21st St

Flushing Meadows-Corona Park, 22. Flushing Bay & Grand Central Pkwy ☎ 718/760-6565

Fort Tilden, 32. Breezy Pt ☎ 718/318-4300

Friends Meeting House, 24. 137-16 Northern Blvd ☎ 718/358-9636

International Design Center, 5. 29,30,31 Thomson Ave ☎ 718/937-7474

Isamu Noguchi Garden Museum, 10. 32-37 Vernon Blvd ☎ 718/204-7088

Jacob Riis Park, 31. Marine Bridge Pkwy at Rockaway Pt Blvd ☎ 718/318-4300

Jamaica Bay Wildlife Refuge, 30. Broad Channel & First Rd ☎ 718/318-4340

Kaufman Astoria Studios, 8. 34-12 36th St ☎ 718/392-5600

Kissena Park, 23. Rose Ave & Parsons Blvd ☎ 718/353-1047

NY Hall of Science, 18. 47-01 111th St ☎ 718/699-0005

MAP 37

Outer Boroughs Listed Alphabetically (Cont.)

QUEENS SITES (cont.)

PS 1 Museum, 4. 46-01 21st St
☎ 718/784-2084

Queens Botanical Gardens, 21.
43-50 Main St ☎ 718/886-3800

Queens Historical Society, 26.
143-35 37th Ave ☎ 718/939-0647

Queens Museum, 20. Flushing
Meadows -Corona Park ☎ 718/592-5555

Silvercup Studios, 3. 42-25 21st St
☎ 718/361-6188

St Demitrios, 11. 30-11 30th Dr
☎ 718/728-1718

St John's University, 29.
Grand Central & Utopia Pkwys
☎ 718/990-6161

Weeping Beech Tree, 27.
37th Ave & Parsons Blvd

West Side Tennis Club, 28.
1 Tennis Pl ☎ 718/268-2300

World's Fair Ice Skating Rink, 19.
Flushing Meadows-Corona Park
☎ 718/271-1996

QUEENS RESTAURANTS

Café Vernon, 2. Vernon Blvd
☎ 718/472-9694. Italian. $$

Elias Corner, 14. 31st St & 24th Ave
☎ 718/932-1510. Seafood. $

Jai Ya Thai, 16. 88-11 Broadway
☎ 718/651-1330. Thai. $

Karyatis, 9. 35-03 Broadway
☎ 718/204-0666. Greek. $

Park Side, 17. 107-01 Corona Ave
☎ 718/271-9274. Italian. $$

Piccola Venezia, 15. 42-01 28th Ave
☎ 718/721-8470. Italian. $

Roumeli Taverna, 13. 33-04 B'way
☎ 718/278-7533. Greek. $

Water's Edge Restaurant, 1.
44th Dr at East River ☎ 718/482-0033.
Continental. $$

Zenon Taverna Meze House, 12.
34-10 31st Ave ☎ 718/956-0133.
Greek. $

STATEN ISLAND SITES

Alice Austin House, 8. 2 Hylan Blvd
☎ 718/816-4506

Garibaldi-Meucci Museum, 7. 420
Tompkins Ave ☎ 718/442-1608

**Gateway National Recreation
Area, 12.** 26 Miller Field
☎ 718/338-3338

**Jaques Marchais Center of Tibetan
Art, 9.** 338 Lighthouse Ave
☎ 718/987-3478

Museum of Staten Island, 2. 75
Stuyvesant Pl ☎ 718/727-1135

**Richmondtown Restoration, Staten
Island Historical Society, 11.**
441 Clarke Ave ☎ 718/351-1611

Snug Harbor Cultural Center, 4.
1000 Richmond Ter ☎ 718/448-2500

Staten Island Ferry, 1. St George
Station, Richmond Terrace & Hyatt St
☎ 718/390-5241

Staten Island Institute, 3.
75 Stuyvesant Pl ☎ 718/727-1135

Staten Island Zoo, 5. 614 Broadway
☎ 718/442-3100

STATEN ISLAND RESTAURANTS

Arirang, 15. 23A Nelson Ave
☎ 718/966-9600. Oriental. $$$

Marina Cafe, 14. 154 Mansion
Ave ☎ 718/967-3077. American.
$$

Pennyfeathers, 10.
187 New Dorp La
☎ 718/667-9722. Continental. $$

Real Madrid, 6. 2073 Forest Ave
☎ 718/447-7885. Spanish. $$

Windjammer, 13. 141 Mansion Ave
☎ 718/948-5772. Seafood. $$$

MAP 38

$$$$ = *over $50* $$$ = *$30-$50* $$ = *$20-$30* $ = *under $20*
Based on cost per person, excluding drinks, service, and 8 1/4% sales tax.

MAP 39 **Parks/Uptown**

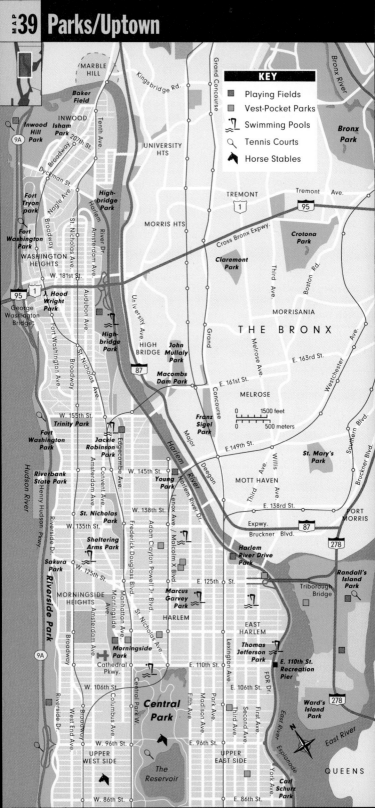

KEY

- Playing Fields
- Vest-Pocket Parks
- Swimming Pools
- Tennis Courts
- Horse Stables

MARBLE HILL

Baker Field

INWOOD

Kingsbridge Rd.

Grand Concourse

Bronx River

Inwood Hill Park

Isham Park

207th St.

Tenth Ave.

UNIVERSITY HTS

Bronx Park

9A

Broadway

Dyckman St.

Nagle Ave.

TREMONT

Tremont Ave.

Fort Tryon park

High-bridge Park

1

95

Fort Washington Park

WASHINGTON HEIGHTS

MORRIS HTS

Crotona Park

Claremont Park

St. Nicholas Ave.

Amsterdam Ave.

River Dr.

Cross Bronx Expwy.

Harlem

W. 181st St.

MORRISANIA

95 1

Hood Wright Park

Third Ave.

THE BRONX

George Washington Bridge

University Ave.

Highbridge Park

Fort Washington Ave.

Broadway

St. Nicholas Ave.

Audubon Ave.

87

HIGH BRIDGE

John Mullaly Park

Grand

E. 163rd St.

Melrose Ave.

Westchester Ave.

Boston Rd.

Macombs Dam Park

E. 161st St.

MELROSE

Southern Blvd.

Hudson River

W. 155th St.

Trinity Park

Fort Washington Park

Franz Sigel Park

Concourse

0   1500 feet

0   500 meters

Jackie Robinson Park

Edgecombe Ave.

Major

E. 149th St.

Willis Ave.

St. Mary's Park

Bruckner Blvd.

Riverbank State Park

Convent Ave.

Amsterdam Ave.

W. 145th St.

Young Park

Harlem

MOTT HAVEN

Deegan

St. Nicholas Park

W. 138th St.

Third Ave.

E. 138th St.

Henry Hudson Pkwy.

Riverside Dr.

Frederick Douglass Blvd.

Adam Clayton Powell Jr. Blvd.

W. 135th St.

Lenox Ave. / Malcolm X Blvd.

River

Expwy.   Bruckner   Blvd.

87

278

PORT MORRIS

Sheltering Arms Park

Sakura Park

W. 125th St.

MORNINGSIDE HEIGHTS

Marcus Garvey Park

HARLEM

Harlem River Drive Park

Randall's Island Park

Triborough Bridge

Riverside Park

Amsterdam Ave.

Morningside Ave.

St. Nicholas Ave.

Manhattan Ave.

E. 125th   St.

EAST HARLEM

9A

Broadway

Morningside Park

Thomas Jefferson Park

E. 110th St. Recreation Pier

Cathedral Pkwy.

E. 110th St.

Lexington Ave.

FDR Dr.

W. 106th St.

Central Park W.

E. 106th St.

Ward's Island Park

278

Columbus Ave.

Central Park

Fifth Ave.

Madison Ave.

Park Ave.

Third Ave.

Second Ave.

First Ave.

East River

West End Ave.

Riverside Dr.

W. 96th St.

E. 96th St.

UPPER EAST SIDE

York Ave.

Esplanade

QUEENS

UPPER WEST SIDE

The Reservoir

UPPER EAST SIDE

Carl Schurz Park

W. 86th St.

E. 86th St.

KEY
- Playing Fields
- Vest-Pocket Parks
- Swimming Pools
- Tennis Courts
- Horse Stables
- Marinas

MAP **41** Central Park/North

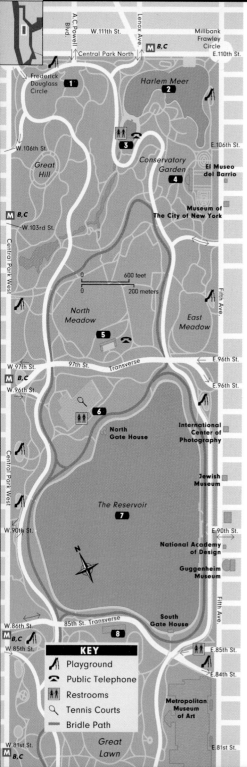

A.C. Powell Blvd

W. 111th St.

Lenox Ave

Millbank Frawley Circle

W. Central Park North

E.110th St.

M B,C

Frederick Douglass Circle

1

W.106th St.

Harlem Meer

2

3

Conservatory Garden

E.106th St.

4

El Museo del Barrio

Great Hill

M B,C

W. 103rd St.

Museum of The City of New York

Central Park West

0   600 feet

0   200 meters

North Meadow

East Meadow

Fifth Ave

5

W. 97th St.

97th St.   Transverse

E. 96th St.

M B,C

W. 96th St.

E. 96th St.

6

North Gate House

International Center of Photography

Central Park West

Jewish Museum

The Reservoir

7

W. 90th St.

E. 90th St.

National Academy of Design

N

Guggenheim Museum

South Gate House

W. 86th St.   85th St. Transverse

Fifth Ave

M B,C

W. 85th St.

8

E. 85th St.

E. 84th St.

KEY

Playground

Public Telephone

Restrooms

Tennis Courts

Bridle Path

Metropolitan Museum of Art

W. 81st St.

Great Lawn

E. 81st St.

M B,C

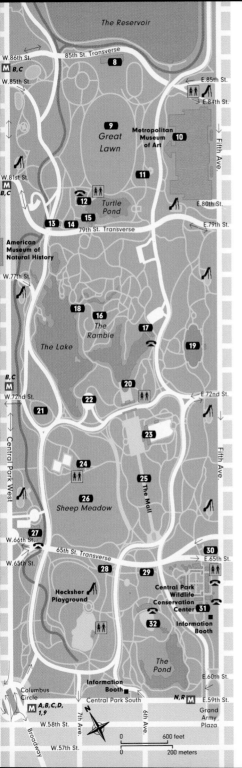

MAP 43 Stadiums & Arenas

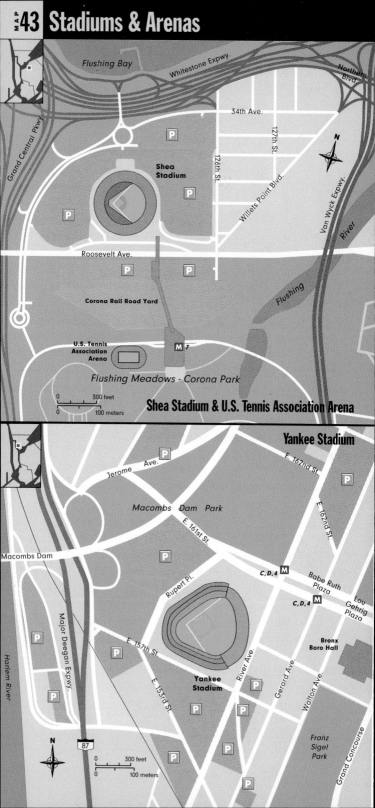

Flushing Bay

Whitestone Expwy.

Northern Blvd.

34th Ave.

127th St.

126th St.

N

Grand Central Pkwy.

Shea Stadium

P

P

P

Willets Point Blvd.

Van Wyck Expwy.

River

Roosevelt Ave.

P

P

Corona Rail Road Yard

Flushing

U.S. Tennis Association Arena

M 7

Flushing Meadows - Corona Park

0   300 feet
0   100 meters

Shea Stadium & U.S. Tennis Association Arena

Yankee Stadium

P

Jerome   Ave.

E. 162nd St.

P

Macombs   Dam   Park

E. 162nd St.

E. 161st St.

Macombs Dam

P

C, D, 4   M   Babe Ruth Plaza

Rupert Pl.

C, D, 4   M   Lou Gehrig Plaza

Major Deegan Expwy.

P

E. 157th St.

Bronx Boro Hall

Harlem River

P

River Ave.

Gerard Ave.

Walton Ave.

P

E. 155th St.

Yankee Stadium

P

P

P

N

87

Franz Sigel Park

Grand Concourse

0   300 feet
0   100 meters

P

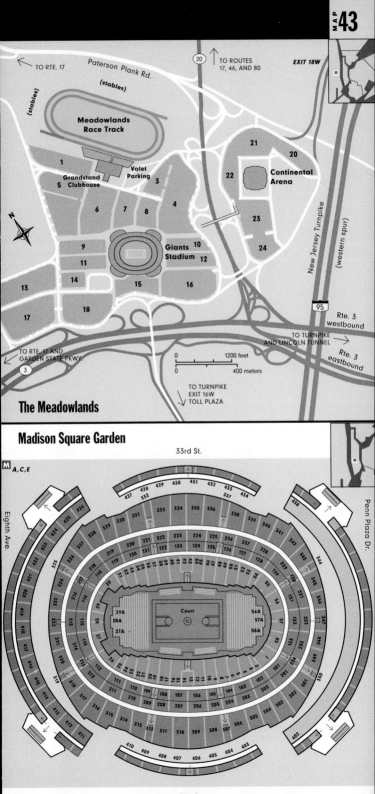

MAP 43

The Meadowlands

TO RTE. 17

Paterson Plank Rd.

TO ROUTES 17, 46, AND 80

EXIT 18W

(stables)

(stables)

Meadowlands Race Track

1

Valet Parking

Grandstand Clubhouse

5

3

6   7   8

4

N

9

11

10

Giants Stadium

12

13

14

15

16

17

18

21

22

Continental Arena

20

23

24

New Jersey Turnpike

(western spur)

95

Rte. 3 westbound

TO TURNPIKE AND LINCOLN TUNNEL

Rte. 3 eastbound

TO RTE. 17 AND GARDEN STATE PKWY.

3

1200 feet

400 meters

TO TURNPIKE EXIT 16W TOLL PLAZA

Madison Square Garden

33rd St.

M A, C, E

Eighth Ave.

Penn Plaza Dr.

427 428 429 430 431 432 433 434

426 332 335 334 335 336 337 436 435

425 424 331 330 551 333 554 335 336 338 339 340 341 344

423 329 328 220 221 222 225 224 225 226 227 228 345 343

422 327 326 219 120 121 122 123 124 125 126 127 229 346 342

421 325 324 218 119 35 36 37 38 39 40 41 42 43 44 128 230 347

420 323 217 118 34 45 46 47 48 49 50 129 231

419 322 216 117 33 30 31 27 51 52 53 130 348

418 321 215 116 29A 56A 54 232

417 320 214 28A 28 Court 57A 55 349 233

416 319 114 27A 58A 56 133 350 234

415 318 213 26 57 57 134 301 207

414 317 212 25 24 23 22 21 20 19 18 17 16 15 14 13 12 11 10 09 08 101 102 103 104 105 302 206 235

413 316 211 111 110 109 108 107 106 105 104 103 102 501 502 503 504 505 506 303 205

412 315 314 313 312 311 310 309 308 307 306 305 304 204

411 410 409 408 407 406 405 404 403 402 203 202 201

31st St.

MAP 44 **Shopping Highlights**

MAP **44**

Listed Alphabetically

ABC Carpet & Home, 27.
888 Broadway ☎ 473–3000

Balducci's, 32. 424 Sixth Ave
☎ 673–2600

Barneys NY, 7. 660 Madison Ave
☎ 826–8900

Barneys NY, 28. 106 Seventh Ave
☎ 929–9000

Bed, Bath & Beyond, 26.
620 Sixth Ave ☎ 255–3550

Bergdorf Goodman, 9. 754 Fifth Ave
☎ 753–7300

Bloomingdale's, 11. 1000 Third Ave
☎ 355–5900

Brooks Brothers, 21.
346 Madison Ave ☎ 682–8800

Canal Jean, 42. 504 Broadway
☎ 226–1130

Century 21, 48. 22 Cortlandt St
☎ 227–9092

Daffy's, 29. 111 Fifth Ave ☎ 529–4477

Dean & Deluca, 41. 560 Broadway
☎ 431–1691

F.A.O. Schwarz, 8. 767 Fifth Ave
☎ 644–9400

575 Fifth Ave, 20. 575 Fifth Ave
☎ 972–4865

Fortunoff, 16. 681 Fifth Ave
☎ 758–6660

Henri Bendel, 15. 712 Fifth Ave
☎ 247–1100

Kam Man, 45. 200 Canal St
☎ 571–0330

Li-Lac Chocolates, 36. 120
Christopher St ☎ 242–7374

Lord & Taylor, 22. 424 Fifth Ave
☎ 391–3344

Macy's, 23. Herald Sq & 34th St
☎ 695–4400

Manhattan Art & Antiques Center, 12.
1050 Second Ave ☎ 355–4400

Manhattan Mall, 24.
Sixth Ave & 33rd St ☎ 465-0500

Museum of Modern Art (Shop), 17.
11 W 53rd St ☎ 708–9700

Patricia Field, 35. 10 E Eighth St
☎ 254–1699

Pearl Paint, 44. 308 Canal St
☎ 431–7932

Petrossian, 10. 182 W 58th St
☎ 245–2217

Polo/Ralph Lauren, 5.
867 Madison Ave ☎ 606–2100 &
888 Madison Ave ☎ 434–8000

Rockefeller Center, 18.
30 Rockefeller Plaza ☎ 632–3975

Saks Fifth Ave, 19. 611 Fifth Ave
☎ 753–4000

South Street Seaport, 50.
Waterfront, Fulton & South Sts
☎ 732–7678

Stern's, 24. Sixth Ave & 33rd St
☎ 244-6060

The Strand, 31. 828 Broadway
☎ 473–1452

Syms, 49. 42 Trinity Pl ☎ 797–1199

Tiffany & Co, 13. 727 Fifth Ave
☎ 755–8000

Tower Records, 3. 2107 Broadway
☎ 799–2500

Tower Records, 4. 1535 Third Ave
☎ 369–2500

Tower Records, 38. 692 Broadway
☎ 505–1500

Trump Tower, 14. 725 Fifth Ave
☎ 832–2000

Urban Outfitters, 34. 374 Sixth Ave
☎ 677–9350

Urban Outfitters, 40. 628 Broadway
☎ 475–0009

World Financial Center, 46.
Waterfront, at West & Vesey Sts
☎ 945–0505

World Trade Center, 47.
West & Vesey Sts ☎ 435–4170

Zabar's, 1. 2245 Broadway
☎ 787–2000

MARKETS

**Annex Antiques Fair & Flea
Market, 25.** Sixth Ave,
betw 25th & 26th Sts. Open Sat, Sun

Canal Market, 43. 370 Canal St.
Open Sat, Sun

Orchard St, 39. Orchard St, betw
Houston & Canal Sts

PS 183 Market, 6. 67th St betw York &
First Aves. Open Sat

PS 41 Market, 33. Greenwich Ave &
Charles St. Open Sat

PS 44 Market, 2. Columbus Ave
betw 76th & 77th Sts. Open Sun

Tower Market, 37. B'way betw W 4th
& Great Jones Sts. Open Sat, Sun

MAP 45 **Shopping/Madison Avenue**

MAP 45

Listed Alphabetically

America Hurrah Antiques, 29.
766 Madison Ave ☎ 535-1930

Andrea Carrano, 8. 850 Madison Ave
☎ 570-1443

Ann Taylor, 41. 645 Madison Ave
☎ 832-9114

Baccarat, 43. 625 Madison Ave
☎ 826-4100

Bally of Switzerland, 45.
628 Madison Ave ☎ 751-9082

Balogh Jewels, 19. 798 Madison Ave
☎ 517-9440

Barneys NY, 37. 660 Madison Ave
☎ 826-8900

Barry Friedman, 6. 851 Madison Ave
☎ 794-8950

Billy Martin's, 17. 812 Madison Ave
☎ 861-3100

Bottega Veneta, 42.
635 Madison Ave ☎ 371-5511

Calvin Klein, 36. 654 Madison Ave
☎ 292-9000

Christofle, 35. 680 Madison Ave
☎ 308-9390

Coach Store, 33. 710 Madison Ave
☎ 319-1772

DeLorenzo, 3. 958 Madison Ave
☎ 249-7575

E Braun & Co, 31. 717 Madison Ave
☎ 838-0650

Emanuel Ungaro, 20.
792 Madison Ave ☎ 249-4090

Erica Wilson, 31. 717 Madison Ave
☎ 832-7290

Florian Pappa, 2. 962 Madison Ave
☎ 288-6770

Fred Leighton, 27. 773 Madison Ave
☎ 288-1872

Georg Jensen, 39. 683 Madison Ave
☎ 759-6457

Gianni Versace, 16.
(Men's) 816 Madison Ave ☎ 744-5572
(Women's) 817 Madison Ave
☎ 744-6868

Giorgio Armani, 12.
815 Madison Ave ☎ 988-9191

Godiva Chocolatier, 24.
793 Madison Ave ☎ 249-9444

Goldpfeil, 26. 777 Madison Ave
☎ 644-8000

Gucci, 23. 795 Madison Ave
☎ 535-1014

Jaeger International, 14.
818 Madison Ave ☎ 628-3350

Joan & David, 15.
816 Madison Ave ☎ 772-3970

Julie, 38. 687 Madison Ave
☎ 688-2345

Krizia, 21. 769 Madison Ave
☎ 879-1211

La Bagagerie, 30. 727 Madison Ave
☎ 758-6570

Laura Ashley, 32. 714 Madison Ave
☎ 735-5000

Lederer, 44. 613 Madison Ave
☎ 355-5515

The Limited, 34. 691 Madison Ave
☎ 838-8787

Mabel's, 7. 849 Madison Ave
☎ 734-3263

Madison Ave Bookshop, 9.
833 Madison Ave ☎ 535-6130

Missoni, 13. 836 Madison Ave
☎ 517-9339

Montenapoleone, 25.
789 Madison Ave ☎ 535-2660

North Beach Leather, 28.
772 Madison Ave ☎ 772-0707

Peter Fox, 18. 806 Madison Ave
☎ 744-8340

Pierre Deux, 5. 870 Madison Ave
☎ 570-9343

Polo/Ralph Lauren, 4.
867 Madison Ave ☎ 606-2100 and
888 Madison Ave ☎ 434-8000

Pratesi, 10. 829 Madison Ave
☎ 288-2315

Sherry Lehmann Inc, 40.
679 Madison Ave ☎ 838-7500

Thomas K Woodard, 22.
799 Madison Ave ☎ 794-9404

Valentino, 11. 825 Madison Ave
☎ 744-0200

Yves St Laurent, 46.
543 Madison Ave ☎ 832-7100

Wicker Garden's Baby, 1.
1327 Madison Ave ☎ 410-7001

MAP 46 Shopping/Fifth Avenue & 57th Street

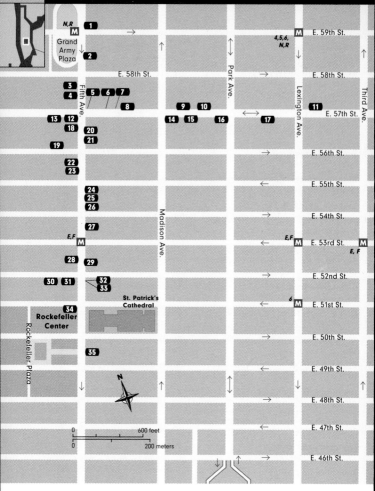

Listed by Site Number

1. A La Vielle Russie
2. F.A.O. Schwarz
3. Bergdorf Goodman
4. Van Cleef & Arpels
5. Warner Bros Studio Store
6. Chanel
7. Burberrys
8. Hermès
9. Prada
10. Louis Vuitton
11. Hammacher Schlemmer
12. Bulgari
12. Israel Sack
12. Mikimoto
13. Charivari 57
14. Victoria's Secret
15. Buccellati
16. Dunhill
16. Hoya Crystal
17. Dempsey & Carroll
18. Fendi
19. Norma Kamali OMO
20. Tiffany & Co
21. Salvatore Ferragamo Men's
21. Salvatore Ferragamo Women's
21. Trump Tower
22. Harry Winston
23. Henri Bendel
24. Godiva
25. Bijan
26. Gucci
27. Fortunoff
28. Botticelli
29. Cartier
30. Traveller's Bookstore
31. Liz Claiborne
32. Mark Cross
33. H Stern
34. Movado
35. Saks Fifth Ave

MAP 46

Listed Alphabetically

A La Vielle Russie, 1. 781 Fifth Ave
☎ 752-1727

Bergdorf Goodman, 3. 754 Fifth Ave
☎ 753-7300

Bijan, 25. 699 Fifth Ave ☎ 758-7500

Botticelli, 28. 666 Fifth Ave
☎ 582-2984

Buccellati, 15. 46 E 57th St
☎ 308-5533

Bulgari, 12. 730 Fifth Ave ☎ 315-9000

Burberrys, 7. 9 E 57th St ☎ 371-5010

Cartier, 29. 653 Fifth Ave ☎ 753-0111

Chanel, 6. 5 E 57th St ☎ 355-5050

Charivari 57, 13. 18 W 57th St
☎ 333-4040

Dempsey & Carroll, 17. 110 E 57th St
☎ 486-7526

Dunhill, 16. 450 Park Ave
☎ 753-9292

F.A.O. Schwarz, 2. 767 Fifth Ave
☎ 644-9400

Fendi, 18. 720 Fifth Ave ☎ 767-0100

Fortunoff, 27. 681 Fifth Ave
☎ 758-6660

Godiva, 24. 701 Fifth Ave
☎ 593-2845

Gucci, 26. 685 Fifth Ave ☎ 826-2600

H Stern, 33. 645 Fifth Ave
☎ 688-0300

Hammacher Schlemmer, 11.
147 E 57th St ☎ 421-9000

Harry Winston, 22. 718 Fifth Ave
☎ 245-2000

Henri Bendel, 23. 712 Fifth Ave
☎ 247-1100

Hermès, 8. 11 E 57th St ☎ 751-3181

Hoya Crystal, 16. 450 Park Ave
☎ 223-6335

Israel Sack, 12. 730 Fifth Ave
☎ 399-6562

Liz Claiborne, 31. 650 Fifth Ave
☎ 956-6505

Louis Vuitton, 10. 49 E 57th St
☎ 371-6111

Mark Cross, 32. 645 Fifth Ave
☎ 421-3000

Mikimoto, 12. 730 Fifth Ave
☎ 586-6992

Movado, 34. 630 Fifth Ave
☎ 262-2059

Norma Kamali OMO, 19.
11 W 56th St ☎ 957-9797

Prada, 9. 45 E 57th St
☎ 308-2332

Saks Fifth Ave, 35. 611 Fifth Ave
☎ 753-4000

Salvatore Ferragamo Men's, 21.
725 Fifth Ave ☎ 246-6211

Salvatore Ferragamo Women's, 21.
725 Fifth Ave ☎ 759-3822

Tiffany & Co, 20. 727 Fifth Ave
☎ 755-8000

Traveller's Bookstore, 30.
22 W 52nd St ☎ 664-0995

Trump Tower, 21. 725 Fifth Ave
☎ 832-2000

Van Cleef & Arpels, 4. 744 Fifth Ave
☎ 644-9500

Victoria's Secret, 14. 34 E 57th St
☎ 758-5592

Warner Bros Studio Store, 5.
1 E 57th St ☎ 754-0300

MAP 47 **Shopping/Upper West Side**

MAP 47

Listed Alphabetically

Acker Merrall & Condit, 25.
160 W 72nd St ☎ 787-1700

Alice Underground, 17.
380 Columbus Ave ☎ 724-6682

Ann Taylor, 31. 2017 Broadway
☎ 873-7344

Aris Mixon & Co, 15.
381 Amsterdam Ave ☎ 724-6904

Avventura, 6. 463 Amsterdam Ave
☎ 769-2510

The Ballet Shop, 33. 1887 Broadway
☎ 581-7990

Barnes & Noble, 5.
2289 Broadway ☎ 362-8835

Betsey Johnson, 27.
248 Columbus Ave ☎ 362-3364

Charivari-72, 30. 257 Columbus Ave
☎ 787-7272

Filene's Basement, 12.
2220 Broadway ☎ 873-8000

Frank Stella Ltd, 9.
440 Columbus Ave ☎ 877-5566

Greenstone and Cie, 8.
442 Columbus Ave ☎ 580-4322

Gryphon Record Shop, 23.
251 W 72nd St ☎ 874-1588

IS 44 Market, 18. Columbus Ave
between 76th & 77th Sts

Laura Ashley, 14. 398 Columbus Ave
☎ 496-5110

Mason's Tennis Mart, 35.
911 Seventh Ave ☎ 757-5374

Morris Brothers, 3. 2322 Broadway
☎ 724-9000

Murder Ink, 1. 2486 Broadway
☎ 362-8905

**Museum of American Folk Art
Gift Shop, 32.** 2 Lincoln Sq
☎ 496-2966

Only Hearts, 16. 386 Columbus Ave
☎ 724-5608

Penny Whistle Toys, 7.
448 Columbus Ave ☎ 873-9090

Petrossian, 34. 182 W 58th St ☎
245-0303

Pottery Barn, 21.
2109 Broadway ☎ 595-5573

Sacco, 19. 324 Columbus Ave
☎ 799-5229

Savage Jewelry, 29.
267 Columbus Ave ☎ 724-4662

Shakespeare & Co, 10.
2259 Broadway ☎ 580-7800

Star Magic, 22.
275 Amsterdam Ave ☎ 769-2020

Sweet Sensations, 28.
275 Columbus Ave ☎ 724-0364

Tip Top, 24. 155 W 72nd St
☎ 787-4960

To Boot, 26. 256 Columbus Ave
☎ 724-8249

Tower Records, 20. 2107 Broadway
☎ 799-2500

Uncle Futz, 13. 408 Amsterdam Ave
☎ 799-6723

Welcome Home Antiques, 2.
562 Columbus Ave ☎ 362-4293

West Side Kids, 4.
498 Amsterdam Ave ☎ 496-7282

Zabar's, 11. 2245 Broadway
☎ 787-2000

MAP 48 **Shopping/Downtown**

Listed Alphabetically

ABC Carpet, 20. 888 Broadway
☎ 473-3000

After the Rain, 76.
149 Mercer St ☎ 431-1044

Agnès B., 74. 116 Prince St
☎ 925-4649

An American Craftsman, 46.
317 Bleecker St ☎ 727-0841

Anna Sui, 84. 113 Greene St
☎ 941-8406

Antique Boutique, 54. 712 Broadway
☎ 460-8830

Armani Exchange, 80. 568 Broadway
☎ 431-6000

Art Boutique, 69. 456 W Broadway
☎ 674-1616

Back Pages Antiques, 75.
125 Greene St ☎ 460-5998

Balducci's, 35. 424 Sixth Ave
☎ 673-2600

Banana Republic, 23.
89 Fifth Ave ☎ 366-4691

Banana Republic, 64.
205 Bleecker St ☎ 473-9570

Barami Studio, 14. 119 Fifth Ave
☎ 529-2300

Barnes & Noble, 21. 105 Fifth Ave
☎ 675-5500

Barnes & Noble, 53. 4 Astor Pl
☎ 420-1322

Barneys NY, 7. 106 Seventh Ave
☎ 593-7800

Bed, Bath, & Beyond, 5.
620 Sixth Ave ☎ 255-3550

Bertha Black, 94. 80 Thompson St
☎ 966-7116

Betsey Johnson, 68. 130 Thompson St
☎ 420-0169

BFO, 12. 149 Fifth Ave ☎ 254-0059

Big Drop, 93. 174 Spring St
☎ 966-4299

Biography Bookstore, 39.
400 Bleecker St ☎ 807-8655

Bird Jungle, 38. 401 Bleecker St
☎ 242-1757

The Body Shop, 51. 747 Broadway
☎ 979-2944

Bombay Company, 17.
900 Broadway ☎ 420-1315

Canal Jean, 100. 504 Broadway
☎ 226-1130

Century 21, 105. 22 Cortlandt St
☎ 227-9092

Ceramica, 92. 59 Thompson St
☎ 941-1307

Comme des Garçons, 86.
116 Wooster St ☎ 219-0660

Common Ground, 36.
19 Greenwich Ave ☎ 989-4178

Daffy's, 16. 111 Fifth Ave ☎ 529-4477

Dean & DeLuca, 81. 560 Broadway
☎ 431-1691

DOM USA, 95. 382 W Broadway
☎ 334-5580

Elan's, 62. 345 Lafayette St
☎ 529-2724

Emporio Armani, 24. 110 Fifth Ave
☎ 727-3240

EMS, 77. 611 B'way ☎ 505-9860

Eneira Downtown, 59. 48 1/2 E 7th St
☎ 473-2454

Enchanted Forest, 99. 85 Mercer St
☎ 925-6677

Fishs Eddy, 19. 889 Broadway
☎ 420-9020

Fishs Eddy, 40. 551 Hudson St
☎ 627-3956

Freelance, 73. 124 Prince St
☎ 925-6641

French Connection, 88.
435 W Broadway ☎ 219-1197

Gourmet Garage, 98. 453 Broome St
☎ 941-5850

Guggenheim Gift Shop, 78. 575
Broadway ☎ 360-3500

Harriet Love, 72. 126 Prince St
☎ 966-2280

Herman's, 28. 860 Broadway
☎ 505-9533

Hold Everything, 8. 104 Seventh Ave
☎ 633-1674

Hyde Park Antiques, 31.
836 Broadway ☎ 477-0033

Ibiza, 34. 46 University Pl
☎ 533-4614

Joan & David, 26. 104 Fifth Ave
☎ 627-1780

Joanie James, 60. 117 E 7th St
☎ 505-9653

Joovay, 89. 436 W Broadway
☎ 431-6386

Just Bulbs, 13. 936 Broadway
☎ 228-7820

MAP 48

MAP 49 Restaurants/Midtown

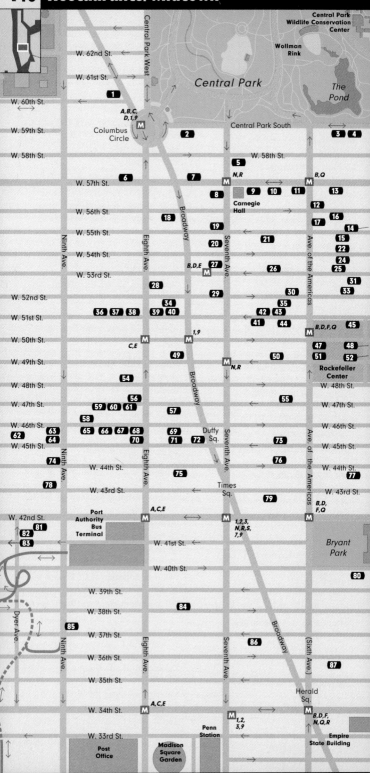

MAP 49

E. 63rd St.

B,Q
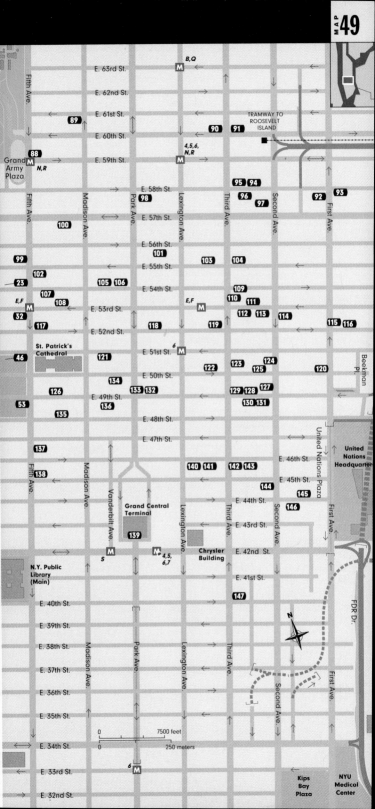

E. 62nd St.

E. 61st St.

89

E. 60th St.

90 **91**

TRAMWAY TO
ROOSEVELT
ISLAND

88

*4,5,6,
N,R*

Grand
Army
Plaza

E. 59th St.

N,R

E. 58th St.

95 **94**

98

96

97

92 **93**

E. 57th St.

100

E. 56th St.

99

101

103 **104**

23

102

105 **106**

E. 55th St.

107

E. 54th St.

109

E,F

108

110 **111**

32

E,F

112 **113**

114

115 **116**

117

E. 53rd St.

118

119

E. 52nd St.

St. Patrick's
Cathedral

6

121

E. 51st St.

46

122

123

124

125

120

E. 50th St.

134

126

133 **132**

129 **128** **127**

53

E. 49th St.

130 **131**

135

136

E. 48th St.

E. 47th St.

137

140 **141**

142 **143**

E. 46th St.

138

144

E. 45th St.

145

Grand Central
Terminal

146

E. 44th St.

United
Nations
Headquarter

139

E. 43rd St.

*4,5,
6,7*

Chrysler
Building

E. 42nd St.

N.Y. Public
Library
(Main)

E. 41st St.

E. 40th St.

147

E. 39th St.

E. 38th St.

E. 37th St.

E. 36th St.

E. 35th St.

0   7500 feet

0   250 meters

E. 34th St.

E. 33rd St.

6

Kips
Bay
Plaza

NYU
Medical
Center

E. 32nd St.

Fifth Ave.
Madison Ave.
Park Ave.
Lexington Ave.
Third Ave.
Second Ave.
First Ave.
Vanderbilt Ave.
Beekman Pl.
United Nations Plaza
FDR Dr.

MAP 49 **Restaurants/Midtown**

Listed by Site Number

1 Gabriel's
2 San Domenico
3 Mickey Mantle's
4 Nirvana
5 Petrossian
6 Le Bar Bat
7 Hard Rock Café
8 Trattoria dell'Arte
9 Russian Tea Room
10 Planet Hollywood
11 Motown Café
12 Harley Davidson Café
13 Mangia
14 La Caravelle
15 La Côte Basque
16 Darbar
17 Allegria
18 Indian Pavilion
19 Carnegie Deli
20 Pasta D'Oro
21 Castellano
22 Ciao Europa
23 Aquavit
24 La Bonne Soupe
25 Raphael
26 Remi
27 Stage Deli
28 Caffe Cielo
29 Rosie O'Grady's
30 Ben Benson's
31 China Grill
32 Select
33 21 Club
34 Gallagher's
35 Victor's Cafe 52
36 Café des Sports
37 Rene Pujol
38 Tout Va Bien
39 Bangkok Cuisine
40 Les Pyrénées
41 Ruth's Chris Steakhouse
42 Le Bernardin
43 Palio
44 La Cité
45 Fashion Café
46 The Assembly
47 Lindy's
48 Sea Grill
49 Wally's & Joseph's
50 Iroha
51 Hurley's

52 American Festival Café
53 La Reserve
54 Swiss Inn
55 Dish of Salt
56 B Smith's
57 Pierre au Tunnel
58 Crepes Suzette
59 Barbetta
60 Becco
61 Broadway Joe
62 Mike's American Bar and Grill
63 Zen Palate
64 Film Center Café
65 Le Rivage
66 Joe Allen's
67 Orso
68 Beefsteak Charlie's
69 Pergola
70 Kodama
71 Frankie & Johnny's
72 Charley O's
73 Cabana Carioca
74 Westbank Café
75 Sardi's
76 Café Un Deux Trois
77 44
78 Le Madeleine
79 Century Cafe
80 Bryant Park Grill
81 Chez Josephine
82 Good Diner
83 World Yacht Cruises
84 Lou G Siegel
85 Market Café
86 Hideaway
87 Keen's
88 Harry Cipriani
89 Mad 61
90 Yellowfingers
91 Arizona 206
92 Rosa Mexicano
93 March
94 Felidia
95 Dawat
96 Tre Scalini
97 Les Sans-Culottes
98 Akbar
99 Adrienne
100 5757
101 Benihana of Tokyo
102 Lespinasse

103 Shun Lee Palace
104 PJ Clarke's
105 Oceana
106 Cellini
107 San Pietro
108 Seryna
109 Vong
110 Lipstick Cafe
111 Il Nido
112 Solera
113 Maple Garden Duckhouse
114 Eamonn Doran
115 Billy's
116 Le Perigord
117 La Grenouille
118 Four Seasons
119 Nippon
120 Wylie's Ribs & Co
121 Tsukiji Sushisay
122 Tatou
123 Al Bustan
124 Zarela
125 Lutèce
126 Sushiden
127 San Giusto
128 David K's
129 Smith & Wollensky
130 Chin Chin
131 Box Tree
132 Inagiku
133 Peacock Alley
134 Giambelli
135 Hatsuhana
136 Dolce
137 Rusty Staub's
138 Morton's of Chicago
139 Grand Central Oyster Bar
140 Nanni
141 Christ Cella
142 Captain's Table
143 Spark's Steakhouse
144 Palm
145 Ambassador Grill
146 Sichuan Pavilion
147 Dock's on Third

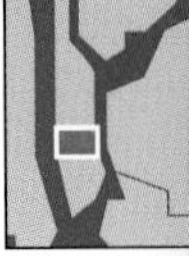

MAP 49

Listed Alphabetically

Adrienne, 99. 700 Fifth Ave
☎ 903-3918. Continental. $$$

Allegria, 17. 66 W 55th St
☎ 956-7755. Italian. $$$

Aquavit, 23. 13 W 54th St ☎ 307-7311.
Scandinavian. $$$$

Akbar, 98. 475 Park Ave ☎ 838-1717.
Indian. $$

Al Bustan, 123. 827 Third Ave
☎ 759-5933. Lebanese. $$

Ambassador Grill, 145. UN
Plaza–Park Hyatt ☎ 702-5014.
Continental. $$

American Festival Café, 52.
Rockefeller Center, 20 W 50th St
☎ 246-6699. American. $$

Arizona 206, 91. 206 E 60th St
☎ 838-0440. Southwestern. $$

The Assembly, 46. 16 W 51st St
☎ 581-3580. Steakhouse. $$$

B Smith's, 56. 771 Eighth Ave
☎ 247-2222. Continental. $$$

Bangkok Cuisine, 39. 885 Eighth Ave
☎ 581-6370. Thai. $$

Barbetta, 59. 321 W 46th St
☎ 246-9171. Italian. $$$

Becco, 60. 355 W 46th St
☎ 397-7597. Italian. $$

Beefsteak Charlie's, 68. 709 Eighth
Ave ☎ 767-8333. Steakhouse. $

Ben Benson's, 30. 123 W 52nd St
☎ 581-8888. Steakhouse. $$$

Benihana of Tokyo, 101. 120 E 56th St
☎ 593-1627. Japanese. $$

Billy's, 115. 948 First Ave
☎ 355-8920. American. $$

Box Tree, 131. 250 E 49th St
☎ 593-9810. Continental. $$$$

Broadway Joe, 61. 315 W 46th St
☎ 246-6513. American. $$

Bryant Park Grill, 80. 25 W 40th St
☎ 840-6500. American. $$

Cabana Carioca, 73. 123 W 45th St
☎ 581-8088. Brazilian. $$

Café des Sports, 36. 329 W 51st St
☎ 974-9052. French. $$

Café Un Deux Trois, 76. 123 W 44th
St ☎ 354-4148. French. $$

Caffe Cielo, 28. 881 Eighth Ave
☎ 246-9555. Italian. $$

Captain's Table, 142. 860
Second Ave ☎ 697-9538.
Seafood. $$

Carnegie Deli, 19. 854 Seventh Ave
☎ 757-2245. Deli. $$

Castellano, 21. 138 W 55th St
☎ 664-1975. Italian. $$$

Cellini, 106. 65 E 54th St ☎ 751-1555.
Italian. $$$

Century Cafe, 79. 132 W 43rd St
☎ 398-1988. American. $$

Charley O's, 72. 218 W 45th St
☎ 626-7300. Continental. $$

Ciao Europa, 22. 63 W 54th St
☎ 247-1200. Italian. $$$

Chez Josephine, 81. 414 W 42nd St
☎ 594-1925. International. $$$

Chin Chin, 130. 216 E 49th St
☎ 888-4555. Chinese. $$

China Grill, 31. 52 W 53rd St
☎ 333-7788. Asian. $$$$

Christ Cella, 141. 160 E 46th St
☎ 697-2479. Steakhouse. $$$$

Crepes Suzette, 58. 363 W 46th St
☎ 581-9717. French. $$$

Darbar, 16. 44 W 56th St ☎ 432-7227.
Indian. $$$

David K's, 128. 209 E 49th St
☎ 486-1800. Chinese. $$

Dawat, 95. 210 E 58th St ☎ 355-7555.
Indian. $$$

Dish of Salt, 55. 133 W 47th St
☎ 921-4242. Cantonese. $$

Dock's on Third, 147. 633 Third Ave
☎ 986-8080. Seafood. $$

Dolce, 136. 60 E 49th St ☎ 692-9292.
Italian. $$$

Eamonn Doran, 114. 998 Second Ave
☎ 752-8088. Continental. $$

Fashion Cafe, 45. 51 Rockefeller
Plaza ☎ 765-3131. American. $$

Felidia, 94. 243 E 58th St ☎ 758-1479.
Italian. $$

5757, 100. 57 E 57th St ☎ 758-5757.
American. $$

Film Center Café, 64. 635 Ninth Ave
☎ 262-2525. American. $

44, 77. 44 W 44th St ☎ 944-8844.
American. $$$

$$$$ = over $50 $$$ = $30–$50 $$ = $20–$30 $ = under $20
Based on cost per person, excluding drinks, service, and 8 1/4% sales tax.

MAP 49 | Restaurants/Midtown

Listed Alphabetically (Cont.)

Four Seasons, 118. 99 E 52nd St ☎ 754-9494. Continental. $$$$

Frankie & Johnny's, 71. 269 W 45th St ☎ 997-9494. American. $$$

Gabriel's, 1. 11 W 60th St ☎ 956-4600. Italian. $$$

Gallagher's, 34. 228 W 52nd St ☎ 245-5336. Steakhouse. $$$

Giambelli, 134. 46 E 50th St ☎ 688-2760. Italian. $$$$

Good Diner, 82. 554 11th Ave ☎ 967-2661. American. $

Grand Central Oyster Bar, 139. Grand Central Terminal ☎ 490-6650. Seafood. $$$

Hard Rock Café, 7. 221 W 57th St ☎ 459-9320. American. $$

Harley Davidson Café, 12. 1370 Ave of the Americas ☎ 245-6000. American. $$

Harry Cipriani, 88. 781 Fifth Ave ☎ 753-5566. Italian. $$$

Hatsuhana, 135. 17 E 48th St ☎ 355-3345. Japanese. $$$

Hideaway, 86. 32 W 37th St ☎ 947-8940. Italian. $$$

Hurley's, 51. 1240 Ave of the Americas ☎ 765-8981. American. $$

Il Nido, 111. 251 E 53rd St ☎ 753-8450. Italian. $$

Inagiku, 132. 111 E 49th St ☎ 355-0440. Japanese. $$$

Indian Pavilion, 18. 240 W 56th St ☎ 489-0035. Indian. $

Iroha, 50. 152 W 49th St ☎ 398-9049. Japanese. $$

Joe Allen's, 66. 326 W 46th St ☎ 581-6464. American. $$

Keen's, 87. 72 W 36th St ☎ 947-3636. Steakhouse. $$$$

Kodama, 70. 301 W 45th St ☎ 582-8065. Japanese. $$

La Bonne Soupe, 24. 48 W 55th St ☎ 586-7650. French. $$

La Caravelle, 14. 33 W 55th St ☎ 586-4252. French. $$$$

La Cité, 44. 120 W 51st St ☎ 956-7100. Steakhouse. $$$

La Côte Basque, 15. 60 W 55th St ☎ 688-6525. French. $$$$

La Grenouille, 117. 3 E 52nd St ☎ 752-1495. French. $$$$

La Reserve, 53. 4 W 49th St ☎ 247-2993. French. $$$

Le Bar Bat, 6. 311 W 57th St ☎ 307-7228. American. $$$

Le Bernardin, 42. 155 W 51st St ☎ 489-1515. Seafood. $$$$

Le Madeleine, 78. 403 W 43rd St ☎ 246-2993. French. $$$

Le Perigord, 116. 405 E 52nd St ☎ 755-6244. French. $$$

Le Rivage, 65. 340 W 46th St ☎ 765-7374. French. $$

Les Pyrénées, 40. 251 W 51st St ☎ 246-0044. French. $$

Les Sans-Culottes, 97. 1085 Second Ave ☎ 838-6660. French. $

Lespinasse, 102. 2 E 55th St ☎ 339-6719. French. $$$$

Lindy's, 47. 1256 Ave of the Americas ☎ 767-8340. Deli. $

Lipstick Cafe, 110. 885 Third Ave ☎ 486-8664. Continental. $$

Lou G Siegel, 84. 209 W 38th St ☎ 921-4433. Kosher. $

Lutèce, 125. 249 E 50th St ☎ 752-2225. French. $$$$

Mad 61, 89. 660 Madison Ave ☎ 833-2200. Italian. $$$

Mangia, 13. 50 W 57th St ☎ 582-5554. Italian. $$

Maple Garden Duckhouse, 113. 236 E 53rd St ☎ 759-8260. Chinese. $

March, 93. 405 E 58th St ☎ 838-9393. American. $$$$

Market Café, 85. 496 Ninth Ave ☎ 967-3989. American. $$

Mickey Mantle's, 3. 42 Central Park S ☎ 688-7777. American. $$

Mike's American Bar and Grill 62. 650 10th Ave ☎ 246-4115. American. $$

Morton's of Chicago, 138. 551 Fifth Ave ☎ 972-3315. Steakhouse. $$

Motown Café, 11. 104 W 57th St ☎ 581-8030. American. $$

Nanni, 140. 146 E 46th St ☎ 697-4161. Italian. $$$

Nippon, 119. 155 E 52nd St ☎ 355-9020. Japanese. $$$

Nirvana, 4. 30 Central Park S ☎ 486-6868. Indian. $$

MAP 49

Listed Alphabetically (cont.)

Oceana, 105. 55 E 54th St
☎ 759-5941. Seafood. $$$$

Orso, 67. 322 W 46th St ☎ 489-7212.
Italian. $$$

Palio, 43. 151 W 51st St ☎ 245-4850.
Italian. $$$$

Palm, 144. 837 Second Ave
☎ 687-2953. Steakhouse. $$$

Pasta D'Oro, 20. 846 Seventh Ave
☎ 586-8096. Italian. $$

Peacock Alley, 133. 301 Park Ave
☎ 872-4895. French. $$$

Pergola, 69. 252 W 46th St
☎ 302-7500. French. $

Petrossian, 5. 182 W 58th St
☎ 245-2214. French. $$$$

Pierre au Tunnel, 57. 250 W 47th St
☎ 575-1220. French. $$

PJ Clarke's, 104. 915 Third Ave
☎ 759-1650. American. $

Planet Hollywood, 10. 140 W 57th St
☎ 333-7827. American. $$$

Raphael, 25. 33 W 54th St
☎ 582-8993. French. $$$

Remi, 26. 145 W 53rd St ☎ 581-4242.
Italian. $$

Rene Pujol, 37. 321 W 51st St
☎ 246-3023. French. $$$

Rosa Mexicano, 92. 1063 First Ave
☎ 753-7407. Mexican. $$$

Rosie O'Grady's, 29. 800 Seventh
Ave ☎ 582-2975. Irish. $$

Russian Tea Room, 9. 150 W 57th St
☎ 265-0947. Russian. $$$

Rusty Staub's, 137. 575 Fifth Ave
☎ 682-1000. American. $$$

Ruth's Chris Steakhouse, 41. 148 W
51st St ☎ 245-9600. American. $$$

San Domenico, 2. 240 Central Park S
☎ 265-5959. Italian. $$$$

San Giusto, 127. 935 Second Ave
☎ 319-0900. Italian. $$$

San Pietro, 107. 18 E 54th St
☎ 753-9015. Italian. $$$

Sardi's, 75. 234 W 44th St
☎ 221-8440. Continental. $$$

Sea Grill, 48. Rockefeller Ctr, 19 W
49th St ☎ 246-9201. Seafood. $$$

Select, 32. 666 Fifth Ave ☎ 757-6662.
American. $$

Seryna, 108. 11 E 53rd St
☎ 980-9393. Japanese. $$$

Shun Lee Palace, 103. 155 E 55th
St ☎ 371-8844. Chinese. $$

Sichuan Palace, 146. 310 E 44th St
☎ 972-7377. Chinese. $$

Smith & Wollensky, 129. 797 Third
Ave ☎ 753-1530. Steakhouse. $$$

Solera, 112. 216 E 53rd St
☎ 644-1166. Spanish. $$$

Spark's Steakhouse, 143. 210 E 46th
St ☎ 687-4855. Steakhouse. $$$

Stage Deli, 27. 834 Seventh Ave
☎ 245-7850. Deli. $

Sushiden, 126. 19 E 49th St
☎ 758-2700. Japanese. $$

Swiss Inn, 54. 311 W 48th St
☎ 459-9280. Swiss. $$$

Tatou, 122. 151 E 50th St ☎ 753-1144.
American. $$$

Tout Va Bien, 38. 311 W 51st St
☎ 265-0190. French. $$

Trattoria dell'Arte, 8. 900 Seventh
Ave ☎ 245-9800. Italian. $$.

Tre Scalini, 96. 230 E 58th St
☎ 688-6888. Italian. $$$

Tsukiji Sushisay, 121. 38 E 51st St
☎ 755-1780. Japanese. $$

21 Club, 33. 21 W 52nd St
☎ 582-7200. Continental. $$$$

Victor's Cafe 52, 35. 236 W 52nd St
☎ 586-7714. Cuban. $$

Vong, 109. 200 E 54th St ☎ 486-9592.
Thai. $$

Wally's & Joseph's, 49. 249 W 49th St
☎ 582-0460. Steakhouse. $$$

Westbank Café, 74. 407 W 42nd St
☎ 695-6909. Continental. $$

World Yacht Cruises, 83. Pier 81, W
41st St ☎ 630-8100. Continental. $$$$

Wylie's Ribs & Co, 120. 891 First Ave
☎ 751-0700. Barbecue. $$

Yellowfingers, 90. 200 E 60th St
☎ 751-8615. Italian. $$

Zarela, 124. 953 Second Ave
☎ 644-6740. Mexican. $$

Zen Palate, 63. 663 Ninth Ave
☎ 582-1669. Vegetarian. $$

$$$$ = *over $50* $$$ = *$30–$50* $$ = *$20–$30* $ = *under $20*
Based on cost per person, excluding drinks, service, and 8 1/4% sales tax.

MAP 50 Restaurants/Upper West Side

MAP **50**

Listed Alphabetically

Bertha's, 18. 2160 Broadway
☎ 362–2500. Mexican. $

Border Cafe, 5. 2637 Broadway
☎ 535–4347. Tex-Mex. $$

Café des Artistes, 29. 1 W 67th St
☎ 877–3500. French. $$$$

Café Luxembourg, 25. 200 W 70th St
☎ 873–7411. American. $$$$

Carmine's, 4. 2450 Broadway
☎ 362–2200. Italian. $$

Conservatory, 41. 15 Central Park W
☎ 581–0896. Continental. $$$

Columbus Bakery, 9. 474 Columbus
Ave ☎ 724–6880. French. $

Dock's Oyster Bar & Grill, 3. 2427
B'way ☎ 724–5588. Seafood. $$$

EJ's Luncheonette, 12.
447 Amsterdam Ave ☎ 873–3444.
American. $

Ernie's, 19. 2150 Broadway
☎ 496–1588. Italian. $$$

Fine & Shapiro, 21. 138 W 72nd St
☎ 877–2874. Deli. $$

Fiorello's Roman Cafe, 38. 1900
Broadway ☎ 595–5330. Italian. $$

Fishin Eddie, 24. 73 W 71st St
☎ 874–3474. Seafood. $$$

Fujiyama Mama, 10. 467 Columbus
Ave ☎ 769–1144. Japanese. $$$

Good Enough to Eat, 7. 483
Amsterdam Ave ☎ 496–0163.
American. $$

Grand Tier, 37. Lincoln Center,
Broadway & W 64th St ☎ 799–3400.
Continental. $$$$

Havana, 22. 240 Columbus Ave
☎ 877–7988. Cuban. $

Houlihan's, 39. 1900 Broadway
☎ 339–8862. American. $$

Iridium, 40. 44 W 63rd St
☎ 582–2121. American. $$$

Isabella's, 17. 359 Columbus Ave
☎ 724–2100. Mediterranean. $$

Isola, 8. 485 Columbus Ave
☎ 362–7400. Italian. $$

John's Pizza, 34. 48 W 65th St
☎ 721–7001. Italian. $

Josephina, 36. 1900 Broadway
☎ 799–1000. American. $$

Josie's, 20. 300 Amsterdam
☎ 769–1212. American, $$

La Boîte en Bois, 27. 75 W 68th St
☎ 874–2705. French. $$$

La Mirabelle, 6. 333 W 86th St
☎ 496–0458. French. $$$

Mackinac Grill, 15. 384
Columbus Ave ☎ 799–1750.
Continental. $$

Museum Cafe, 16. 366 Columbus
Ave ☎ 799–0150. American. $$

O'Neal's, 35. 49 W 64th St
☎ 787–4663. Continental. $$

Panavino, 32. Lincoln Ctr, Broadway
& W 64th St ☎ 874–7000. European. $

Rain, 11. 100 W 82nd St
☎ 501–0776. South Asian. $$

The Saloon, 33. 1920 B'way
☎ 874–1500. American. $$$

Santa Fe, 26. 72 W 69th St
☎ 724–0822. Mexican. $$$

Sarabeth's Kitchen, 13. 423
Amsterdam Ave ☎ 496–6280.
American. $$

Savann, 14. 414 Amsterdam Ave
☎ 580–0202. American. $

Shun Lee West, 31. 43 W 65th St
☎ 595–8895. Chinese. $$

Sidewalkers, 23. 12 W 72nd St
☎ 799–6070. Seafood. $$$

Sylvia's, 2. 328 Lenox Ave
☎ 996–0660. Soul. $$

Tavern on the Green, 30. Central
Park W & 67th St ☎ 873–3200.
Continental. $$$$

Terrace, 1. 400 W 119th St
☎ 666–9490. French. $$$$

Vince & Eddie's, 28. 70 W 68th St
☎ 721–0068. American. $$$

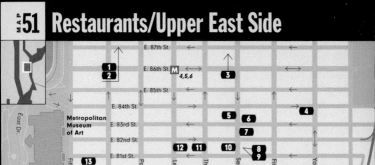

MAP 51 Restaurants/Upper East Side

MAP 51

Listed Alphabetically (cont.)

Aureole, 47. 34 E 61st St ☎ 319-1660. French. $$$$

Bangkok House, 21. 1485 First Ave ☎ 249-5700. Thai. $$

Bistro de Norde, 2. 1312 Madison Ave ☎ 289-0997. French. $$$

Bravo Gianni, 42. 230 E 63rd St ☎ 752-7272. Italian. $$$

Café Crocodile, 30. 354 E 74th St ☎ 249-6619. French. $$$

Canyon Road, 24. 1470 First Ave ☎ 734-1600. Southwestern. $$$

Carlyle Restaurant, 16. Carlyle Hotel, 35 E 76th St ☎ 744-1600. Continental. $$$$

Divino, 8. 1556 Second Ave ☎ 861-1096. Italian. $$$

Dresner's, 25. 1479 York Ave ☎ 988-5153. American. $$

E.A.T., 14. 1064 Madison Ave ☎ 772-0022. Continental. $$$

Elaine's, 3. 1703 Second Ave ☎ 534-8103. Italian. $$$

First Wok, 19. 1374 Third Ave ☎ 861-2600. Chinese. $

Il Valletto, 45. 133 E 61st St ☎ 838-3939. Italian. $$$

JG Melon, 28. 1291 Third Ave ☎ 744-0585. American. $

Jackson Hole, 39. 232 E 64th St ☎ 371-7187. American. $$

Jo Jo, 40. 160 E 64th St ☎ 223-5656. French. $$$

La Metairie, 11. 1442 Third Ave ☎ 988-1800. French. $$$$

La Refuge, 12. 166 La E 82nd St ☎ 861-4505. French. $$$

Le Cirque, 37. 58 E 65th St ☎ 794-9292. French. $$$$

Le Regence, 38. 37 E 64th St ☎ 734-9100. French. $$$$

Lenox Hill Restaurant, 18. 1105 Lexington Ave ☎ 879-9520. American. $

Lusardi's, 20. 1494 Second Ave ☎ 249-2020. Italian. $$$$

Madame Romaine, 44. 132 E 61st St ☎ 758-2422. French. $$

Mark's Restaurant, 15. 25 E 77th St ☎ 879-1864. Continental. $$$

Maxim's, 46. 680 Madison Ave ☎ 751-5111. French. $$$$

Mezzaluna, 29. 1295 Third Ave ☎ 535-9600. Italian. $$$

Mocca, 7. 1588 Second Ave ☎ 734-6470. Hungarian. $$

Pamir, 27. 1437 Second Ave ☎ 650-1095. Afghan. $$

Parioli Romanissimo, 13. 24 E 81st St ☎ 288-2391. Italian. $$$$

Park Avenue Café, 43. 100 E 63rd St ☎ 644-1900. American. $$$

Petaluma, 31. 1356 First Ave ☎ 772-8800. Italian. $$$

Pig Heaven, 9. 1540 Second Ave ☎ 744-4333. Chinese. $$

Polo, 33. Westbury Hotel, 840 Madison Ave ☎ 535-2000. French/Continental. $$$

Post House, 41. 28 E 63rd St ☎ 935-2888. American. $$$

Red Tulip, 26. 439 E 75th St ☎ 734-4893. Hungarian. $$$

Right Bank, 34. 822 Madison Ave ☎ 737-2811. American. $$

Sarabeth's Kitchen-Whitney, 17. 1295 Madison Ave ☎ 410-7335. American. $

Serendipity 3, 48. 225 E 60th St ☎ 838-3531. American. $$

7th Regiment Mess, 35. 643 Park Ave ☎ 744-4107. American. $$

Sign of the Dove, 36. 1110 Third Ave ☎ 861-8080. Continental. $$$

Sistina, 10. 1555 Second Ave ☎ 861-7660. Italian. $$$$

Szechuan Kitchen, 22. 1460 First Ave ☎ 249-4615. Szechuan. $

Table d'Hote, 1. 44 E 92nd St ☎ 348-8125. Continental. $$

Tombola, 5. 1603 Second Ave ☎ 772-2161. Italian. $$$

Trastevere, 6. 309 E 83rd St ☎ 734-6343. Italian. $$

Voulez-Vous, 23. 1462 First Ave ☎ 249-1776. French. $$

Wilkinson's, 4. 1573 York Ave ☎ 535-5454. Seafood. $$$

Zucchini, 32. 1336 First Ave ☎ 249-0559. American. $$

MAP 52 **Restaurants/Chelsea & Gramercy Park**

Listed by Site Number

MAP 52

Listed Alphabetically

Aja, 22. 937 Broadway ☎ 473-8388. American. $$

Albuquerque Eats, 13. 375 Third Ave ☎ 683-6500. Mexican. $

Alva, 20. 36 E 22nd St ☎ 228-4399. American. $$$

America, 27. 9 E 18th St ☎ 505-2110. American. $$$

An American Place, 9. 2 Park Ave ☎ 684-2122. American. $$$$

Bendix, 43. 219 Eighth Ave ☎ 366-0560. Thai/American. $

Bolo, 18. 23 E 22nd St ☎ 228-2200. Italian. $$

Cal's, 35. 55 W 21st St ☎ 929-0740. French. $$$

Canastel's, 24. 233 Park Ave S ☎ 677-9622. Italian. $$$

Charley O's, 1. 9 Penn Plaza ☎ 630-0310. Irish. $$

Chelsea Bistro, 44. 358 W 23rd St ☎ 727-2026. French. $$$

Chelsea Café, 4. 250 W 27th St ☎ 989-3804. Continental. $$

Chelsea Trattoria Italiana, 40. 108 Eighth Ave ☎ 924-7786. Italian. $$$

City Crab, 23. 235 Park Ave S ☎ 529-3800. Seafood. $$

Claire, 37. 156 Seventh Ave ☎ 255-1955. Caribbean. $$

Coffee Shop, 28. 29 Union Sq W ☎ 243-7969. Brazilian. $$

CT, 17. 111 E 22nd St ☎ 995-8500. American. $$

Da Umberto, 33. 107 W 17th St ☎ 989-0303. Italian. $$

Eighteen and Eighth, 42. 159 Eighth Ave ☎ 242-5000. American. $

El Parador, 6. 325 E 34th St ☎ 679-6812. Mexican. $$

Empire Diner, 45. 210 Tenth Ave ☎ 243-2736. American. $$

Estoril Sol, 3. 382 Eighth Ave ☎ 947-1043. Portuguese. $

Fat Tuesday's, 25. 190 Third Ave ☎ 533-7900. American. $

Flowers, 31. 21 W 17th St ☎ 691-8888. Continental. $$$

Hunan Fifth Ave, 8. 323 Fifth Ave ☎ 686-3366. Chinese. $

La Colombe d'Or, 15. 134 E 26th St ☎ 689-0666. French. $$$

La Petite Auberge, 12. 116 Lexington Ave ☎ 689-5003. French. $$

Le Madri, 38. 168 W 18th St ☎ 727-8022. Italian. $$$

Le Parc, 21. Gramercy Park Hotel, 2 Lexington Ave ☎ 475-4320. Continental. $$

Les Halles, 11. 411 Park Ave S ☎ 679-4111. French. $$

Lola, 36. 30 W 22nd St ☎ 675-6700. Caribbean. $$$

Marchi's, 7. 251 E 31st St ☎ 679-2494. Italian. $$$

Merchants NY, 39. 112 Seventh Ave ☎ 366-7267. American. $

Mesa Grill, 30. 102 Fifth Ave ☎ 807-7400. Southwestern. $$

Nicola Paone, 5. 207 E 34th St ☎ 889-3239. Italian. $$$$

Old Homestead, 41. 56 Ninth Ave ☎ 242-9040. Steakhouse. $$

Ole, 16. 434 Second Ave ☎ 725-1953. Spanish. $

Park Ave Country Club, 14. 381 Park Ave S ☎ 685-3636. American. $$$

Park Bistro, 10. 414 Park Ave S ☎ 689-1360. French. $$$

Periyali, 34. 35 W 20th St ☎ 463-7890. Greek. $$$

Rascals, 19. 12 E 22nd St ☎ 420-1777. American. $$

Sal Anthony's, 26. 55 Irving Pl ☎ 982-9030. Italian. $$

San Remo, 2. 393 Eighth Ave ☎ 564-1819. Italian. $

Union Square Café, 29. 21 E 16th St ☎ 243-4020. European. $$$$

Zip City, 32. 3 W 18th St ☎ 366-6333. American. $$

Zucca, 46. 227 10th Ave ☎ 741-1970. Mediterranean. $$

$$$$ = *over $50* $$$ = *$30–$50* $$ = *$20–$30* $ = *under $20*
Based on cost per person, excluding drinks, service, and 8 1/4% sales tax.

MAP 53 Restaurants/The Village & Downtown

Union Square Park

L, N, R, 4, 5, 6

Fifth Ave.

W. 14th St.
W. 13th St.
W. 12th St.
W. 11th St.
W. 10th St.
W. 9th St.
W. 8th St.

MacDougal Alley
Washington Mews

Washington Sq. N.

Washington Square Park

E. Washington Pl.

Waverly Pl.

New York University

W. 3rd St.

Washington Sq. S.

Bleecker St.

W. Houston St.

B, D, F, Q

Grand St.

N, R

Canal St.

Lispenard St.
Walker St.
White St.
Franklin St.
Leonard St.
Worth St.
Thomas St.
Duane St.
Reade St.

Chambers St.
Warren St.
Murray St.
Park Pl.
Barclay St.
Vesey St.

World Trade Center

World Financial Center

World Financial Center

Battery Park City

Hudson River

West Side Highway

Holland Tunnel

Manhattan Community College

Independence Plaza

Holland Tunnel Entrance
Holland Tunnel Exit

St. Luke's Pl.

Sheridan Square

Abingdon Square

City Hall Park

Liberty St.
Cedar St.
Thames St.
Pine St.
Albany
Carlisle
Rector
Wall St.
Exchange Pl.

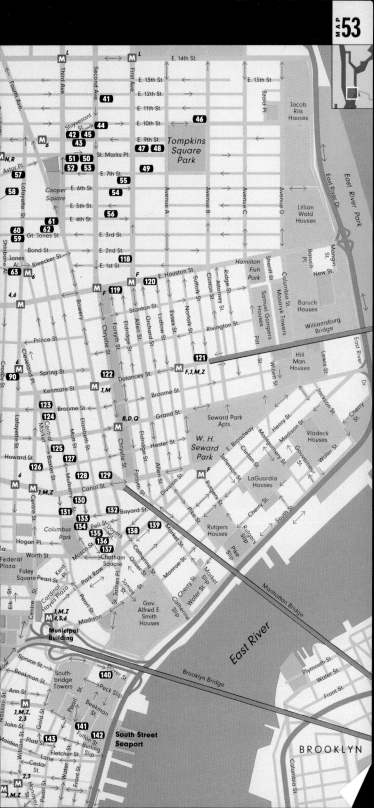

MAP 53

L

M L
E. 14th St.

Third Ave
Second Ave
First Ave
E. 13th St.   E. 13th St.

Szold Pl.

Jacob Riis Houses

Fourth Ave
E. 12th St.

41
E. 11th St.

Stuyvesant
E. 10th St.
44
46

42 45
E. 9th St.
Tompkins Square Park

M 6
43

N,R
51 50
St. Marks Pl.
47 48

52 53
E. 7th St.
49

57
Astor Pl.
55

58
Cooper Square
E. 6th St.
54

Avenue A
Avenue B
Avenue C
Avenue D

East River Park
East River

Lillian Wald Houses

E. 5th St.
56

60 61
E. 4th St.
Lafayette St.

59 62
Gt. Jones St.
E. 3rd St.

Jones Al.
Bond St.
E. 2nd St.

63 6
Bleecker St.
E. 1st St.
118

Hamilton Fish Park

Sheriff St.
Columbia St.

Mangin St.
Baruch Pl.
New St.

4,6
F
119
F
120
E. Houston St.

Suffolk St.
Clinton St.
Ridge St.
Attorney St.

Samuel Gompers Houses

Masaryk Towers
Baruch Houses

Bowery
Stanton St.

Crosby St.
Prince St.
Chrystie St.
Forsyth St.
Eldridge St.
Allen St.
Orchard St.
Ludlow St.
Essex St.
Norfolk St.

Rivington St.
Pitt
St.

Williamsburg Bridge

6
Spring St.
90

Kenmare St.
122
Delancey St.
121
F,J,M,Z
M
Willett St.
Lewis St.

Hill Man. Houses

East River Dr.

123
Broome St.
M J,M
Broome St.

124
B,D,Q

Lafayette St.
Central Market
125
Elizabeth St.
Mott St.
Eldridge St.
Forsyth St.
Hester St.
Grand St.

Seward Park Apts.

E. Broadway
Henry St.
Madison St.
Montgomery St.
Clinton St.
Jefferson St.

Jackson St.
Cherry St.
Water St.
Gouverneur St.

Vladeck Houses

127
Chrystie St.
W. H. Seward Park

Howard St.
126

128
129
Allen St.
Forsyth St.
M F

6
Canal St.
Division St.

M J,M,Z
130
Rutgers St.

LaGuardia Houses

Centre St.
131
132
Bayard St.

South St.
Cherry St.

Columbus Park
133
Pell St.
138
139

134
Doyers
135
Mosco St.
Market St.

Rutgers Houses

136
Oliver St.
Catherine St.
Monroe St.

Rutgers Slip

Hogan Pl.
137
Chatham Square

Worth St.
Park Row
James St.

Pike St.

Pike Slip

Foley Square
Pearl St.
Cardinal Hayes Plaza

Gov. Alfred E. Smith Houses

Market Slip
Water St.
Cherry St.

Elk St.
Centre St.

Federal Plaza

J,M,Z
M 4,5,6
Madison

Manhattan Bridge

Municipal Building

East River

Spruce St.
Beekman St.
Southbridge Towers
140
Dover St.

Ann St.
Peck Slip

Plymouth St.
Water St.
Front St.

M J,M,Z
2,3
John St.
Pearl St.
Beekman St.

141
142
South Street Seaport

Gold St.
William St.
Maiden
143
Fulton St.
Burling Slip
Fletcher St.

Cedar St.
2,3
Water St.
Front St.

BROOKLYN

Columbia St.

M J,M,Z
Hanover

MAP 53 **Restaurants/The Village & Downtown**

MAP **53**

Listed Alphabetically

Abyssinia, 101. 35 Grand St
☎ 226-5959. Ethiopian. $

Acme Bar & Grill, 59. 9 Great Jones
St ☎ 420-1934. Southern. $

Aggie's, 71. 146 W Houston St
☎ 673-8994. American. $

Alison on Dominick Street, 91. 38
Dominick St ☎ 727-1188. French. $$$

American Renaissance, 102. 260 W
Broadway ☎ 343-0049. American. $$$

Angelica Kitchen, 41. 300 E 12th St
☎ 228-2909. Vegetarian. $

Angelo's, 125. 146 Mulberry St
☎ 966-1277. Italian. $$

Around the Clock, 42. 8 Stuyvesant
St ☎ 598-0402. American. $

Arqua, 113. 281 Church St
☎ 334-1888. Italian. $$$

Arturo's, 72. 106 Houston St
☎ 475-9828. Italian. $$

Barocco, 103. 301 Church St
☎ 431-1445. Italian. $$$

Barolo, 94. 398 W Broadway
☎ 226-1102. Italian. $$

Bayamo, 58. 704 Broadway
☎ 475-5151. Cuban/Chinese. $$

Benito's II, 124. 163 Mulberry St
☎ 226-9012. Italian. $$$

Benny's Burritos, 7. 113 Greenwich
Ave ☎ 727-0584. Mexican. $

Berry's, 83. 180 Spring St
☎ 226-4394. American. $$

Black Sheep, 36. 344 W 11th St
☎ 242-1010. French. $$

Bo Ky, 133. 80 Bayard St
☎ 406-2292. Chinese. $

Boca Chica, 118. 13 First Ave
☎ 473-0108. Latin. $$

Boom, 85. 152 Spring St ☎ 431-3663.
Thai/Viet/Cont. $$$

Boxer's, 22. 190 W 4th St
☎ 633-2275. American. $$

Bridge Café, 140. 279 Water St
☎ 227-3344. American. $$

Bubby's, 106. 120 Hudson St
☎ 219-0666. American. $

Café de Bruxelles, 6. 118 Greenwich
Ave ☎ 206-1830. Belgian. $$$

Café Loup, 10. 105 W 13th St
☎ 255-4746. Continental. $$

Café Tabac, 43. 232 E 9th St
☎ 674-7072. American. $$

Canton, 138. 45 Division St
☎ 226-4441. Chinese. $$

Capsouto Frères, 93.
451 Washington St ☎ 966-4900.
French. $$$$

Caribe, 35. 117 Perry St ☎ 255-9191.
Jamaican. $

Casa La Femme, 74. 150 Wooster St
☎ 505-0005. Mediterranean. $$$

Cent' Anni, 28. 50 Carmine St
☎ 989-9494. Italian. $$$

Chanterelle, 108. 2 Harrison St
☎ 966-6960. French. $$$$

Chumley's, 31. 86 Bedford St
☎ 675-4449. American. $

Cottonwood Cafe, 17. 415 Bleecker
St ☎ 924-6271. Southwestern. $

Cucina di Pesce, 56. 87 E 4th St
☎ 260-6800. Italian. $

Cucina Stagionale, 26. 275 Bleecker
St ☎ 924-2707. Italian. $

Cuisine de Saigon, 8. 154 W 13th St
☎ 255-6003. Vietnamese. $$

Cupping Room Cafe, 97. 359 W
B'way ☎ 925-2898. Australian. $$

Da Silvano, 70. 260 Sixth Ave
☎ 982-2343. Italian. $$$

Diva, 98. 349 W B'way
☎ 226-5885. Seafood. $$$

DoJo, 51. 24 St Mark's Pl
☎ 674-9821. American. $

Duane Park Cafe, 110. 157 Duane St
☎ 732-5555. American. $$

Ear Inn, 92. 326 Spring St
☎ 226-9060. American. $$

Ecco, 114. 124 Chambers St
☎ 227-7074. Italian. $$$$

El Rincon de Espana, 67.
226 Thompson St ☎ 475-9891.
Spanish. $$

El Teddy's, 105. 219 W Broadway
☎ 941-7070. Mexican. $

Elephant & Castle, 14. 68 Greenwich
Ave ☎ 243-1400. American. $$

Ennio & Michael, 66. 539 LaGuardia
Pl ☎ 677-8577. Italian. $$

Felix, 99. 340 W Broadway
☎ 431-0021. French. $$

$$$$ = *over $50* $$$ = *$30–$50* $$ = *$20–$30* $ = *under $20*
Based on cost per person, excluding drinks, service, and 8 1/4% sales tax.

Listed Alphabetically (cont.)

Five & Ten No Exaggeration, 86. 77 Greene St ☎ 925-7414. American. $$

Florent, 1. 69 Gansevoort St ☎ 989-5779. French. $$

Fraunces Tavern, 143. 54 Pearl St ☎ 269-0144. American/ Continental. $$$

French Roast, 11. 458 Ave of the Americas ☎ 533-2233. French. $

Gianni's, 141. 15 Fulton St ☎ 608-7300. Italian. $$$

Gotham Bar & Grill, 13. 12 E 12th St ☎ 620-4020. American. $$$$

Great Jones St Cafe, 62. 54 Great Jones St ☎ 674-9304. American. $$

Greenhouse Restaurant & Grill, 117. 3 World Trade Ctr ☎ 938-9100. American. $$

Grotta Azzurra, 123. 387 Broome St ☎ 925-8775. Italian. $$

Harry's Burrito, 49. 91 E 7th St ☎ 477-0773. Mexican. $

Home, 25. 20 Cornelia St ☎ 243-9579. American. $$$

Hudson River Club, 115. 4 World Financial Ctr ☎ 786-1500. American. $$$$

I Tre Merli, 73. 463 W Broadway ☎ 254-8699. Italian. $$$$

Il Cantinori, 39. 32 E 10th St ☎ 673-6044. Italian. $$$

Il Mulino, 64. 86 W 3rd St ☎ 673-3783. Italian. $$$$

Indochine, 57. 430 Lafayette St ☎ 505-5111. Viet/Cambodian. $$$$

Jane St Seafood Cafe, 5. 575 Hudson St ☎ 242-0003. Seafood. $$$$

Japonica, 12. 100 University Place ☎ 243-7752. Japanese. $$

Jean Claude, 75. 137 Sullivan St ☎ 475-9232. French. $$

Jerry's, 88. 101 Prince St ☎ 966-9464. American. $$

John's of Bleecker Street, 27. 278 Bleecker St ☎ 243-1680. Pizza. $

Katz's Delicatessen, 120. 205 E Houston St ☎ 254-2246. Deli. $

Khyber Pass, 50. 34 St Mark's Pl ☎ 473-0989. Afghan. $$

Knickerbocker, 38. 33 University Pl ☎ 228-8490. American. $$

La Boheme, 29. 24 Minetta La ☎ 473-6447. American. $$

La Metairie, 19. 189 W 10th St ☎ 989-0343. French. $$

Le Figaro, 68. 184 Bleecker St ☎ 677-1100. American. $

Le Gamin, 76. 50 MacDougal St ☎ 254-4678. French. $

Le Pactole, 116. 2 World Financial Ctr ☎ 945-9444. French. $$$$

Le Pescadou, 78. 18 King St ☎ 924-3434. French. $$

Life Cafe, 46. 343 E 10th St ☎ 477-8791. Vegetarian. $

Lion's Head, 21. 59 Christopher St ☎ 929-0670. American. $$

Lucky Strike, 100. 59 Grand St ☎ 941-0479. Continental. $$

Mandarin Court, 130. 61 Mott St ☎ 608-3838. Chinese. $$$$

Mappamondo Due, 34. 581 Hudson ☎ 675-7474. Italian. $

Marion's, 61. 354 Bowery ☎ 475-7621. Italian. $$$

McSorley's Old Ale House, 52. 15 E 7th St ☎ 473-9148. American. $

Mezzogiorno, 82. 195 Spring St ☎ 334-2112. Italian. $$$

Mitali East, 54. 334 E 6th St ☎ 533-2508. Indian. $

Montrachet, 104. 239 W Broadway ☎ 219-2777. French. $$$

Moondance Diner, 96. 80 Sixth Ave ☎ 226-1191. American. $

Nice, 139. 35 E Broadway ☎ 406-9510. Chinese. $$

Nobu, 107. 105 Hudson ☎ 219-0050. Japanese. $$$

Noho Star, 63. 330 Lafayette St ☎ 925-0070. American. $

Noodle Town, 132. 28 1/2 Bowery ☎ 349-0923. Chinese. $

Odeon, 112. 145 W Broadway ☎ 233-0507. Continental. $$$

Omen, 81. 113 Thompson St ☎ 925-8923. Japanese. $$

One City Café, 4. 240 W 14th St ☎ 807-1738. American. $$

103, 53. 103 Second Ave ☎ 777-4120. American. $$

One If By Land, Two If By Sea, 23. 17 Barrow St ☎ 228-0822. Continental. $$$$

MAP 53

Listed Alphabetically (cont.)

Patisserie Lanciani, 16. 271 W 4th St
☎ 929-0739. French. $

Peking Duck House, 135. 22 Mott St
☎ 227-1810. Chinese. $$

Pink Tea Cup, 30. 42 Grove St
☎ 807-6755. Soul. $

Po, 24. 31 Cornelia St ☎ 645-2189.
Italian. $$$

Provence, 77. 38 MacDougal St
☎ 475-7500. French. $$$

Puglia, 126. 189 Hester St
☎ 226-8912. Italian. $$

Quantum Leap, 65. 88 W 3rd St
☎ 677-8050. Vegetarian. $$

Raoul's, 80. 180 Prince St
☎ 966-3518. French. $$$$

Ratner's, 121. 138 Delancey St
☎ 677-5588. Kosher. $

Rio Mar, 3. 7 Ninth Ave ☎ 242-1623.
Spanish. $$

Riviera Café, 20. 225 W 4th St
☎ 929-3250. American. $$

Rose Café, 37. 24 Fifth Ave
☎ 260-4118. American. $$

Saigon, 134. 89-91 Bayard St
☎ 732-8988. Vietnamese. $

Salaam Bombay, 111. 317 Greenwich
St ☎ 226-9400. Indian. $$

Sammy's Roumanian, 122.
157 Chrystie St ☎ 673-5526.
Eastern European. $$$$

Sazerac House Bar & Grill, 32. 533
Hudson St ☎ 989-0313. American. $$

**Second Ave Kosher Delicatessen,
44.** 156 Second Ave
☎ 677-0606. Deli. $

Sevilla, 18. 62 Charles St
☎ 243-9513. Spanish. $$

Silver Palace, 129. 52 Bowery
☎ 964-1204. Chinese. $

Sloppy Louie's, 142. 92 South St
☎ 509-9694. Seafood. $$

Soho Kitchen, 87. 103 Greene St
☎ 925-1866. American. $$$

Souen, 79. 28 E 13th St ☎ 627-7150.
Vegetarian. $

Spring St Natural, 90. 62 Spring St
☎ 966-0290. American. $

Stingy Lu Lu's, 48. 129 St Marks Pl
☎ 674-3545. American. $

Telephone Bar & Grill, 45.
149 Second Ave ☎ 529-5000.
Continental. $$

Tennessee Mountain, 84. 143
Spring St ☎ 431-3993. American. $

Teresa's, 55. 103 First Ave
☎ 228-0604. Polish/Deli. $

Thailand, 131. 106 Bayard St
☎ 349-3132. Thai. $

Time Cafe, 60. 380 Lafayette St
☎ 533-7000. American. $$

Tortilla Flats, 2. 767 Washington St
☎ 243-1053. Mexican. $

TriBeCa Grill, 109. 375 Greenwich St
☎ 941-3900. Seafood. $$$

Triplet's Roumanian, 95. 11-17
Grand St ☎ 925-9303. Eastern
European. $$$

20 Mott St, 136. 20 Mott St
☎ 964-0380. Chinese. $$

Villa Mosconi, 69. 69 MacDougal St
☎ 673-0390. Italian. $$

Vincent's Clam Bar, 127. 119 Mott St
☎ 226-8133. Italian. $$

Waverly Coffee Shop, 40. 19
Waverly Pl ☎ 674-3760. American. $

White Horse Tavern, 33. 567 Hudson
St ☎ 243-9260. American. $

Wo Hop, 137. 15 Mott St
☎ 766-9160. Chinese. $

Wong Kee, 128. 113 Mott St
☎ 226-9018. Chinese. $

Yaffa Cafe, 47. 97 St Mark's Pl
☎ 674-9302. Vegetarian. $

Ye Waverly Inn, 15. 16 Bank St
☎ 929-4377. American. $$

Yonah Schimmel's Knishery, 119.
137 E Houston St ☎ 477-2858.
Jewish. $

Zinno, 9. 126 W 13th St
☎ 924-5182. Italian. $$$

Zoe, 89. 90 Prince St
☎ 966-0644. American. $$$

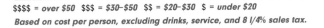

$$$$ = over $50 $$$ = $30–$50 $$ = $20–$30 $ = under $20
Based on cost per person, excluding drinks, service, and 8 1/4% sales tax.

MAP **54** Hotels/Manhattan

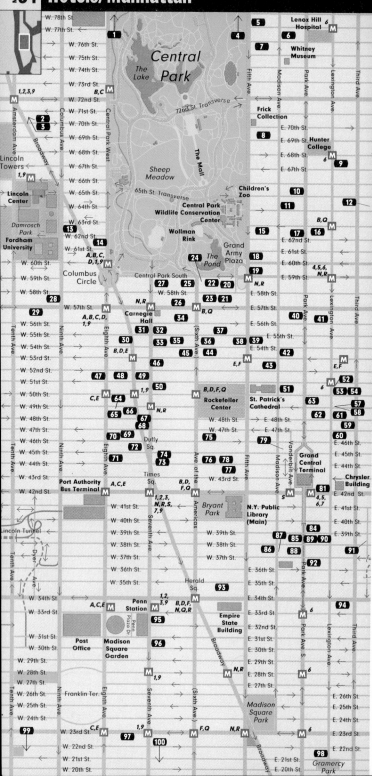

MAP 54

Listed by Site Number

MAP 54 # Hotels/Manhattan

Listed Alphabetically

Algonquin, 76. 59 W 44th St
☎ 840-6800. 📠 944-1419. $$

Ameritania, 30. 1701 B'way
☎ 247-5000. 📠 247-3316. $

Barbizon, 16. 140 E 63rd St
☎ 838-5700. 📠 888-4271. $$

Bedford, 84. 118 E 40th St
☎ 697-4800. 📠 697-1093. $$

Beekman Tower, 56. 3 Mitchell Pl
☎ 355-7300. 📠 753-9366. $$

Best Western, 67. 234 W 48th St
☎ 246-8800. 📠 974-3922. $

Beverly, 54. 125 E 50th St
☎ 753-2700. 📠 753-2700. $

Broadway American, 2. 2178 B'way
☎ 362-1100. 📠 787-9521. $

Carlyle, 6. 35 E 76th St
☎ 744-1600. 📠 717-4682. $$$$

Chatwal Inn, 74. 132 W 45th St
☎ 921-7600. 📠 719-0171. $

Chelsea Hotel, 97. 222 W 23rd St
☎ 243-3700. 📠 243-3700. $

Comfort Inn, 93. 42 W 35th St
☎ 947-0200. 📠 594-3047. $

Consulate, 64. 224 W 49th St
☎ 246-5252. 📠 245-2305. $

Days Hotel, 65. 790 Eighth Avenue
☎ 581-7000. 📠 974-0291. $

Days Inn, 29. 440 W 57th St
☎ 581-8100. 📠 581-8719. $

Doral Court, 90. 130 E 39th St
☎ 685-1100. 📠 889-0287. $$

Doral Inn, 57. 541 Lexington Ave
☎ 755-1200. 📠 319-8344. $

Doral Park, 85. 70 Park Ave
☎ 973-2400. 📠 808-9029. $$$

Doral Tuscany, 89. 120 E 39th St
☎ 687-7050. 📠 7686-1600. $$$

Dorset, 44. 30 W 54th St
☎ 247-7300. 📠 581-0153. $$$

Doubletree Guest Suites, 68. 1568
B'way ☎ 719-1600. 📠 921-5212. $$$$

Drake Swissotel, 40. 440 Park Ave
☎ 421-0900. 📠 371-4190. $$$$

Dumont Plaza, 94. 150 E 34th St
☎ 481-7600. 📠 889-8856. $$

Eastgate Tower, 91. 222 E 39th St
☎ 687-8000. 📠 490-2634. $$

Edison, 69. 228 W 47th St
☎ 840-5000. 📠 596-6868. $

Elysee, 42. 60 E 54th St
☎ 753-1066. 📠 980-9278. $$

Essex House, 27. 160 Central Park S
☎ 247-0300. 📠 315-1839. $$$$

Excelsior, 1. 45 W 81st St
☎ 362-9200. 📠 721-2994. $

Fitzpatrick, 9. 687 Lexington Ave
☎ 355-0100. 📠 355-1371. $$

Gorham, 35. 136 W 55th St
☎ 245-1800. 📠 245-1800. $

Gramercy Park, 98. 2 Lexington Ave
☎ 475-4320. 📠 505-0535. $

Grand Hyatt NY, 81. Park Ave & 42nd
St ☎ 883-1234. 📠 697-3772. $$$$

Helmsley Middletowne, 59. 148 E
48th St ☎ 755-3000. 📠 832-0261. $$

Helmsley Windsor, 21. 100 W 58th St
☎ 265-2100. 📠 315-0371. $$

Holiday Inn Crowne Plaza, 66. 1605
B'way ☎ 977-4000. 📠 333-7393. $$

Hotel Beacon, 3. 2130 B'way
☎ 787-1100. 📠 724-0839. $

Hotel Iroquois, 78. 49 W 44th St
☎ 840-3080. 📠 398-1754. $$

Hotel Wentworth, 75. 59 W 46th St
☎ 719-2300. 📠 768-3477. $

Howard Johnson, 47. 851 Eighth Ave
☎ 581-4100. 📠 974-7502. $

Inter-Continental NY, 62. 111 E 48th
St ☎ 755-5900. 📠 644-0079. $$$

Kitano, 88. 66 Park Ave ☎ 681-6007.
📠 885-7100. $

Lexington, 61. 511 Lexington Ave
☎ 755-4400. 📠 751-4091. $$

Loews New York, 52. 569 Lexington
Ave ☎ 752-7000. 📠 758-6311. $$

Lombardy, 41. 111 E 56th St
☎ 753-8600. 📠 754-5683. $$

Lowell, 15. 28 E 63rd St ☎ 838-1400.
📠 319-4230. $$$$

Lyden Gardens, 12. 215 E 64th St
☎ 355-1230. 📠 319-4230. $$

Lyden House, 55. 320 E 53rd St
☎ 888-6070. 📠 935-7690. $$

Madison Towers, 86. 22 E 38th St
☎ 685-3700. 📠 447-0747. $$

The Mark, 5. 25 E 77th St
☎ 744-4300. 📠 744-2749. $$$$

Marriott East Side, 58. 525 Lexington
Ave ☎ 755-4000. 📠 751-3440. $$

Marriott Marquis, 72. 1535 B'way
☎ 398-1900. 📠 704-8930. $$$$

Mayfair, 10. 610 Park Ave
☎ 288-0800. 📠 737-0538. $$$$

Mayflower, 14. I5 Central Park W
☎ 265-0060. 📠 265-5098. $$$

MAP **54**

Listed Alphabetically (cont.)

Michelangelo, 50. 152 W 51st St
☎ 765-1900. 🖷 541-6604. $$$$

Milford Plaza, 71. 270 W 45 St
☎ 869-3600. 🖷 944-8357. $

Millennium, 100. 55 Church St
☎ 693-2001. 🖷 571-2316. $$$

Millennium Broadway, 73. 145 W
44th St ☎ 768-4400. 🖷 768-0847. $$$

Morgans, 87. 237 Madison Ave
☎ 686-0300. 🖷 779-8352. $$

NY Helmsley, 82. 212 E 42nd St
☎ 490-8900. 🖷 936-4792. $$$$

NY Hilton, 45. 1335 Ave of the Americas
☎ 586-7000. 🖷 315-1374. $$$$

NY Palace, 51. 455 Madison Ave
☎ 888-7000. 🖷 303-6000. $$$$

NY Hotel Pennsylvania, 95. 401
Seventh Ave ☎ 736-5000.
🖷 502-8799. $$

NY Vista, 99. 3 World Trade Ctr
☎ 938-9100. 🖷 444-3444. $$$$

Novotel, 48. 226 W 52nd St
☎ 315-0100. 🖷 765-5369. $$

Omni Berkshire Place, 43. 21 E 52nd
St ☎ 800/790-1900. 🖷 308-9473. $$$$

Omni Park Central, 31. 870 Seventh
Ave ☎ 247-8000. 🖷 484-3374. $$

Paramount, 70. 235 W 46th St
☎ 764-5500. 🖷 354-5237. $

Park Lane, 22. 36 Central Park S
☎ 371-4000. 🖷 319-9065. $$$$

Parker Meridien, 34. 119 W 56th St
☎ 245-5000. 🖷 307-1776. $$$$

The Peninsula, 38. 700 Fifth Ave
☎ 247-2200. 🖷 903-3949. $$$$

Pierre, 18. 2 E 61st St
☎ 838-8000. 🖷 940-8109. $$$$

The Plaza, 20. Fifth Ave & 59th St
☎ 759-3000. 🖷 759-3167. $$$$

Plaza Athénée, 11. 37 E 64th St
☎ 734-9100. 🖷 772-0958. $$$$

Plaza Fifty, 53. 155 E 50th St
☎ 751-5710. 🖷 753-1468. $$

Radisson Empire, 13. 44 W 63rd St
☎ 265-7400. 🖷 315-0349. $

Regency, 17. 540 Park Ave
☎ 759-4100. 🖷 826-5674. $$$$

Rihga Royal, 33. 151 W 54th St
☎ 307-5000. 🖷 765-6530. $$$$

Ritz-Carlton, 25. 112 Central
Park S ☎ 757-1900.
🖷 757-9620. $$$$

Roger Smith Winthrop, 60. 501 Lex
Ave ☎ 755-1400. 🖷 319-9130. $

Roosevelt, 79. 45 E 45th St
☎ 661-9600. 🖷 687-5064. $$

Royalton, 77. 44 W 44th St
☎ 869-4400. 🖷 869-8965. $$$

St Regis, 39. 2 E 55th St ☎ 753-4500.
🖷 787-3447. $$$

Salisbury, 26. 123 W 57th St
☎ 246-1300. 🖷 977-7752. $

Sheraton Center, 46. 811 Seventh
Ave ☎ 581-1000. 🖷 262-4410. $$$

Sheraton Manhattan Hotel, 49.
790 Seventh Ave ☎ 581-3300.
🖷 582-5489. $$

Sheraton Park Ave, 92. 45 Park Ave
☎ 685-7676. 🖷 889-3193. $$$$

Sherry Netherland, 19. 781 Fifth Ave
☎ 355-2800. 🖷 832-4845. $$$$

Shoreham, 37. 33 W 55th St
☎ 247-6700. 🖷 765-9741. $

Southgate Tower, 96. 371 Seventh
Ave ☎ 563-1800. 🖷 643-8028. $$$

St Moritz, 24. 50 Central Park S
☎ 755-5800. 🖷 751-2952. $$$$

Stanhope, 4. 995 Fifth Ave
☎ 288-5800. 🖷 517-0088. $$$$

The Surrey, 7. 20 E 76th St
☎ 288-3700. 🖷 628-1549. $$$

Tudor, 83. 304 E 42nd St
☎ 986-8800. 🖷 986-1758. $$$

UN Plaza, 80. 1 UN Plaza
☎ 758-1234. 🖷 702-5051. $$$$

Waldorf-Astoria, 63. 301 Park Ave
☎ 355-3000. 🖷 872-7272. $$$$

Warwick, 36. 65 W 54th St
☎ 247-2700. 🖷 957-8915. $$$

Wellington, 32. 871 Seventh Ave
☎ 247-3900. 🖷 581-1719. $

Westbury, 8. 15 E 69th St
☎ 535-2000. 🖷 535-5058. $$$

Westpark Hotel, 28. 308 W 58th St
☎ 246-6440. 🖷 246-3131. $

Wyndham, 23. 42 W 58th St
☎ 753-3500. 🖷 754-5638. $

$$$$ = *over $260* $$$ = *$200–$260* $$ = *$160–$200* $ = *under $160*
*All prices are for a standard double room, excluding 13 1/4% city and state sales
tax and $2 occupancy tax.*

MAP 55 **Performing Arts**

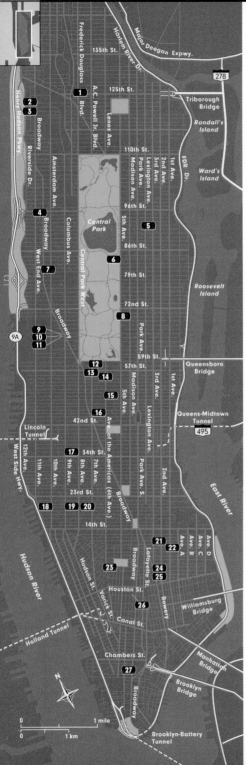

MAP **55**

Listed Alphabetically

Amato Opera, 25. 319 Bowery
☎ 228-8200

Apollo Theater, 1. 253 W 125th St
☎ 749-5838

Beacon Theater, 7. 2124 Broadway
☎ 496-7070

CAMI Hall, 12. 165 W 57th St
☎ 841-9650

Carnegie Hall, 13. 154 W 57th St
☎ 247-7800

City Center, 14. 131 W 55th St
☎ 581-7907

Dance Theatre Workshop, 20.
219 W 19th St ☎ 924-0077

**Grace Rainey Rogers Auditorium,
6.** Metropolitan Museum,
1000 Fifth Ave ☎ 570-3949

Joyce Theater, 19. 175 Eighth Ave
☎ 242-0800

Juilliard School, 9. 60 Lincoln Ctr
Plaza ☎ 799-5000

Kaufman 92nd St YMCA, 5.
1395 Lexington Ave ☎ 415-5440

The Kitchen, 18. 512 W 19th St
☎ 255-5793

La MaMa ETC, 24. 74A E 4th St
☎ 475-7710

Lincoln Center, 10. Broadway &
64th St ☎ 875-5000

Madison Square Garden, 17.
Seventh Ave & 32nd St ☎ 465-6000

Manhattan School of Music, 2.
120 Claremont Ave ☎ 749-2802

Merkin Concert Hall, 11.
129 W 67th St ☎ 362-8719

Music Room, 8.
Frick Museum, 1 E 70th St ☎ 288-0700

**New Museum of Contemporary
Art, 26.** 583 Broadway ☎ 219-1222

PS 122, 22. 150 First Ave ☎ 477-5288

Radio City Music Hall, 15.
1260 Sixth Ave ☎ 247-4777

Riverside Church, 3. 490 Riverside Dr
☎ 222-5900

St Mark's-in-the-Bowery, 21.
Second Ave & 10th St ☎ 674-6377

Symphony Space, 4. 2537 Broadway
☎ 864-5400

Town Hall, 16. 123 W 43rd St
☎ 840-2824

Warren St Performance Loft, 27.
46 Warren St ☎ 732-3149

Washington Square Church, 23.
135 W 4th St ☎ 777-2528

Lincoln Center

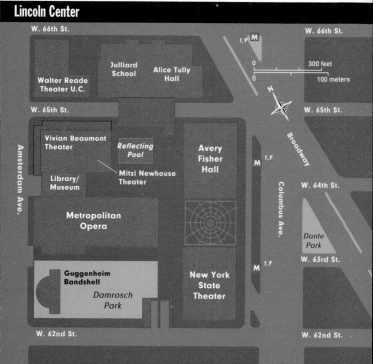

MAP 56 Theater District

Listed Alphabetically

Ambassador, 10. 215 W 49th St
☎ 239-6200

American Place, 20. 111 W 46th St
☎ 840-2960

Belasco, 37. 111 W 44th St
☎ 239-6200

Booth, 32. 222 W 45th St ☎ 239-6200

Broadhurst, 35. 235 W 44th St
☎ 239-6200

Broadway, 4. 1681 Broadway
☎ 239-6200

Brooks Atkinson, 16. 256 W 47th St
☎ 719-4099

Circle in the Square, 9. 1633
Broadway ☎ 307-2700

City Center Stage II, 1. 131 W 55th St
☎ 581-1212

Cort, 14. 138 W 48th St ☎ 239-6200

Criterion Center, 24. 1530 Broadway
☎ 239-6200

Douglas Fairbanks, 45.
432 W 42nd St ☎ 239-4321

Ensemble Studio Theatre, 3.
549 W 52nd St ☎ 247-3405

Ethel Barrymore, 15. 243 W 47th St
☎ 239-6200

Eugene O'Neill, 11. 230 W 49th St
☎ 239-6200

45th St, 27. 354 W 45th St ☎ 957-8757

Gershwin, 7. 222 W 51st St
☎ 586-6510

Golden, 29. 252 W 45th St
☎ 239-6200

Harold Clurman, 48. 412 W 42nd St
☎ 594-2370

Helen Hayes, 39. 240 W 44th St
☎ 944-9450

Imperial, 22. 249 W 45th St
☎ 239-6200

John Houseman, 43. 450 W 42nd St
☎ 967-9077

Judith Anderson, 46. 412 W 42nd St
☎ 564-7853

Kaufman, 42. 534 W 42nd St
☎ 563-1684

Lamb's, 40. 130 W 44th St
☎ 997-1780

Longacre, 12. 220 W 48th St
☎ 239-6200

Lunt-Fontanne, 18. 205 W 46th St
☎ 575-9200

Lyceum, 26. 149 W 45th St
☎ 239-6200

Majestic, 34. 247 W 44th St
☎ 239-6200

Marquis, 25. 211 W 45th St
☎ 382-0100

Martin Beck, 28. 302 W 45th St
☎ 239-6200

Minskoff, 33. Broadway & 45th St
☎ 869-0550

Music Box, 23. 239 W 45th St
☎ 239-6200

Nat Horne, 44. Ninth Ave & 42nd St
☎ 279-4200

Nederlander, 50. 208 W 41st St
☎ 921-8000

Neil Simon, 6. 250 W 52nd St
☎ 757-8646

Palace, 17. Broadway & 47th St
☎ 730-8200

Playwrights Horizons, 47.
416 W 42nd St ☎ 279-4200

Plymouth, 31. 236 W 45th St
☎ 239-6200

Richard Rogers, 21. 226 W 46th St
☎ 221-1211

Roundabout, 19. 1530 Broadway
☎ 869-8400

Royale, 30. 242 W 45th St
☎ 239-6200

St James, 38. 246 W 44th St
☎ 239-6200

Samuel Beckett, 49. 412 W 42nd St
☎ 594-2826

Shubert, 36. 225 W 44th St
☎ 239-6200

Theatre Four, 2. 424 W 55th St
☎ 757-3900

Virginia, 5. 245 W 52nd St
☎ 239-6200

Walter Kerr, 13. 219 W 48th St
☎ 239-6200

Westside Theatre, 41. 407 W 43rd St
☎ 315-2244

Winter Garden, 8. 1634 Broadway
☎ 239-6200

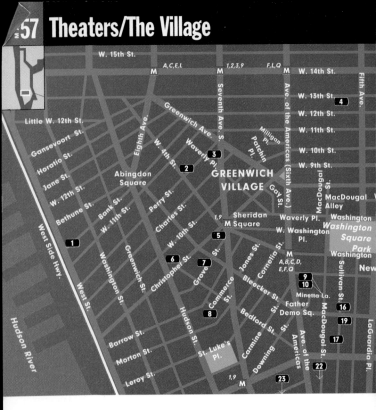

MAP 57

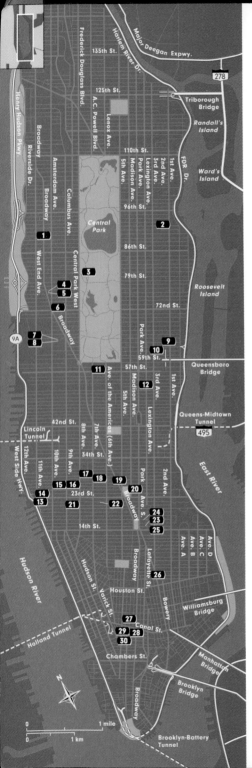

MAP 58

Listed Alphabetically

Atlantic Theater Company, 21.
336 W 20th St ☎ 645-1242

Bouwerie Lane Theatre, 26.
330 Bowery ☎ 677-0060

Chicago City Limits, 9. 1105 1st Ave
☎ 888-5233

Delacorte, 3. 81st St in Central Park
☎ 861-7283

Franklin Furnace, 28. 112 Franklin St
☎ 925-4671

Gramercy Arts, 20. 138 E 27th St
☎ 889-2850

Hudson Guild, 15. 441 W 26th St
☎ 760-9800

Manhattan Class Co, 18.
120 W 28th St ☎ 727-7722

Manhattan Theatre Club, 11.
131 W 55th St ☎ 645-5590

Mitzi Newhouse, 7. Lincoln Center,
Broadway & W 64th St ☎ 362-7600

One Dream, 30. 232 W B'way
☎ 274-1450

Performing Garage, 27.
33 Wooster St ☎ 966-3651

Playhouse 91, 2. 316 E 91st St
☎ 831-2000

Promenade, 5. 2162 Broadway
☎ 580-1313

Sanford Meisner, 13.
164 Eleventh Ave ☎ 206-1764

Second Stage, 4. Broadway & 76th St
☎ 873-6103

SoHo Rep, 29. 46 Walker St
☎ 977-5955

Susan Bloch, 16. 307 W 26th St
☎ 633-9797

TADA!, 18. 120 W 28th St ☎ 627-1732

Theatre East, 10. 211 E 60th St
☎ 838-9090

Triad, 6. 158 W 72nd St ☎ 362-2590

29th St, 17. 212 W 29th St ☎ 465-0575

UBU Rep, 19. 15 W 28th St
☎ 679-7562

Union Square Theatre, 24.
100 E 17th St ☎ 505-0700

Variety Arts, 25. Third Ave & 14th St
☎ 239-6200

Village, 22. 133 W 22nd St
☎ 627-8411

Vineyard Theatre, 23. 108 E 15th St
☎ 353-3366

Vivian Beaumont, 8. Lincoln
Center, Broadway & W 64th St
☎ 362-7600

WPA, 14. 519 W 23rd St ☎ 206-0523

York, 12. 619 Lexington Ave
☎ 935-5820

59

Listed Alphabetically

Angelika 57, 28. 225 W 57th St
☎ 586-1900

Astor Plaza, 41. Broadway &
44th St ☎ 869-8340

Baronet & Coronet, 24.
993 Third Ave ☎ 355-1663

Beekman, 15. 1254 Second Ave
☎ 737-2622

Carnegie Hall Cinemas, 26.
887 Seventh Ave ☎ 265-2520

Carnegie Screening Room, 27.
887 Seventh Ave ☎ 757-2131

Chelsea Cinemas (1-9), 49.
260 W 23rd St ☎ 691-4744

Cinema 1, 2 & Cinema 3rd Ave, 21.
Third Ave & 60th St ☎ 753-6022

Cinema 3, 23. 2 W 59th St
☎ 752-5959

Columbus Circle, 19. Broadway &
61st St ☎ 247-5070

Criterion Center (1-7), 42.
1514 Broadway ☎ 354-0900

Crown Gotham Cinema, 31.
969 Third Ave ☎ 759-2262

Eastside Playhouse, 33. 919 Third
Ave ☎ 755-3020

84th St Sixplex, 3. 2310 Broadway
☎ 877-3600

86th St East Twin, 6. 210 E 86th St
☎ 249-1144

Embassy I, 39. Broadway & 46th St
☎ 302-0494

Embassy 2-4, 40. 701 Seventh Ave
☎ 730-7262

59th St East Cinema, 22.
259 E 59th St ☎ 759-4630

First & 62nd Cinemas (1-6), 20.
400 E 62nd St ☎ 752-4600

Gemini 1 & 2, 16. 1210 Second Ave
☎ 832-1670

Guild, 38. 33 W 50th St ☎ 757-2406

Lincoln Plaza Cinemas (1-6), 17.
B'way & 63rd St ☎ 757-2280

Lincoln Square, 9. 1992 Broadway
☎ 336-5000

Loews NY Twin, 14. 1271 Second Ave
☎ 744-7339

Manhattan Twin, 25.
Third Ave & 59th St ☎ 935-6420

Metro Cinema 1 & 2, 1. Broadway &
99th St ☎ 222-1200

Movieplex, 42, 44. 244 W 42nd St
☎ 997-7522

Murray Hill Cinemas (1-4), 45.
160 E 34th St ☎ 689-6548

Museum of Modern Art, 35.
11 W 53rd ☎ 708-9480

National Twin, 43.
1500 Broadway ☎ 869-0950

Naturemax, 8. American Museum of
Natural History, Central Park W &
80th St ☎ 769-5650

Olympia I & II, 2.
Broadway & 107th St ☎ 865-8128

Orpheum VII, 4. 1538 Third Ave
☎ 876-2400

Paris, 29. 4 W 58th St ☎ 980-5656

Park & 86th St Cinemas I & II, 5.
125 E 86th St ☎ 534-1880

Plaza, 30. 42 E 58th St ☎ 355-3320

Radio City Music Hall, 37. Sixth Ave
& 50th St ☎ 247-4777

Regency, 10. 1987 Broadway
☎ 724-3700

68th St Playhouse, 13.
Third Ave & 68th St ☎ 734-0302

62nd & Broadway, 18. Broadway &
62nd St ☎ 265-7466

Sutton I & II, 32. Third Ave & 57th St
☎ 759-1411

34th St East, 47. Second Ave &
34th St ☎ 683-0255

34th St Showplace, 46.
Third Ave & 34th St ☎ 532-5544

Tower East, 11. Third Ave & 72nd St
☎ 879-1313

23rd St West Triplex, 48.
333 W 23rd St ☎ 989-0060

United Artist East, 7. First Ave &
85th St ☎ 249-5100

Whitney Museum, 12.
Third Ave & 68th St ☎ 570-0537

Worldwide Cinemas (1-6), 36.
Eighth Ave & 50th St ☎ 246-1583

Ziegfeld Theatre, 34.
Sixth Ave & 54th St ☎ 765-7600

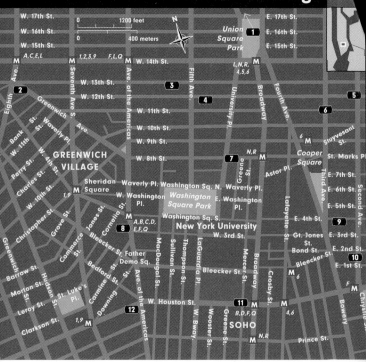

Nightlife/Uptown

MAP 6

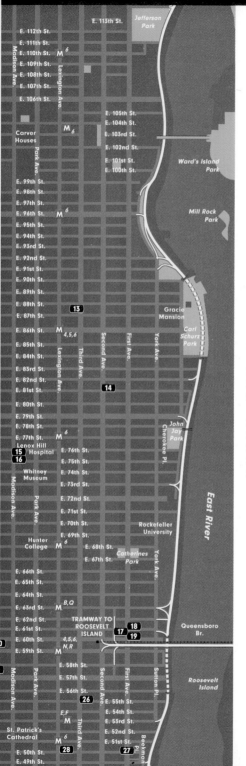

W. 50th St.

W. 49th St.

W. 48th St.

C,E M *1,9* M *B,D,F,Q*

St. Patrick's Cathedral

Rockefeller Center

Fifth Ave.

Madison Ave.

Vanderbilt Ave.

Grand Central Terminal

N,R

W. 47th St. **35**

W. 46th St. **36 37**

Duffy Sq.

Ave. of the Americas

32 33

34

38

W. 45th St.

W. 44th St.

W. 43rd St. **40**

Times Sq. **43 44**

45

39

W. 42nd St.

41 *A,C,E* M **42**

B,D,
F,Q

E. 38th St.

Lincoln Tunnel

W. 41st St.

W. 40th St.

1,2,3
N,R,S,
7,9

Bryant Park

N.Y. Public Library (Main)

46

Port Authority Bus Terminal

Ninth Ave.

Eighth Ave.

Seventh Ave.

E. 37th St.

E. 36th St.

E. 35th St.

Park Ave.

Lexington Ave.

47

Jacob K. Javits Convention Center

W. 37th St.

W. 36th St.

W. 35th St.

W. 34th St.

Dyer Ave.

Herald Sq. *B,D,F,*

N,Q,R

E. 34th St.

E. 33rd St. M *6*

52

W. 33rd St.

W. 32nd St.

Post Office

A,C,E M

1,2,
3,9

Empire State Building

E. 32nd St.

E. 31st St.

E. 30th St.

W. 31st St.

Madison Square Garden

Penn Plaza Dr.

Broadway

Penn Station

(Sixth Ave.)

48

E. 29th St.

M *1,9*

E. 28th St. M *6*

W. 30th St.

W. 29th St.

W. 28th St.

W. 27th St.

N,R M

Eleventh Ave.

Tenth Ave.

Franklin Ter.

Madison Square Park

Park Ave. S.

W. 26th St.

W. 25th St.

W. 24th St. **53**

Flatiron Building

E. 20th St.

54

W. 23rd St. *C,E* M *1,9* M *F,Q* M *N,R* M

W. 22nd St.

W. 21st St.

Eighth Ave.

Ninth Ave.

Seventh Ave.

61

58 59

57 60

Fifth Ave.

55

56

W. 20th St.

W. 19th St.

W. 18th St.

E. 19th St.

62

63 Union Square Park **72**

West Side Hwy.

W. 17th St.

W. 16th St. **68**

67

E. 16th St.

E. 15th St. **73**

L,N,R,
4,5,6

4th Ave.

Broadway

W. 15th St.

69 *1,2,3,9*

F,L,Q M

65 66

W. 14th St. *A,C,E,L* M **70**

W. 13th St.

71

Seventh Ave.

W. 12th St.

W. 11th St.

E. 13th St.

E. 12th St.

E. 11th St.

76

E. 9th Street

University Pl.

75

Little W. 12th St.

Gansevoort St.

Horatio St.

Jane St.

77

79 78

W. 10th St.

W. 9th St.

E. 8th St.

84 *N,R*

Greenwich Ave.

Ave. of the Americas

Hudson River

W. 12th St.

Bethune St.

Bank St.

Abingdon Square

Perry St.

Charles St.

80

Greenwich St.

Washington St.

Sheridan Sq. *1,9* M

Washington Square Park

Astor Pl.

Lafayette St.

Greene St.

86

W. 11th St.

83

81

82

A,B,C,D,
E,F,Q M

LaGuardia Pl.

105

Great Jones St.

West St.

Christopher St.

Grove St.

Bleecker St.

89

87

90

91

95

W. 3rd St.

Bleecker St.

Bond St.

6

Barrow St.

Morton St.

Leroy St.

Bedford St.

99

92

93

94

Sullivan St.

MacDougal St.

4,6

Clarkson St.

W. Houston St.

98 *B,D,F,Q*

St. Luke's Pl.

Carmine St.

Downing St.

Thompson St.

N,R M

SOHO

King St.

W. Houston St. *1,9*

100

Hudson St.

Charlton St. *C,E* M

Varick St.

West Broadway

Wooster St.

Greene St.

Mercer St.

Crosby St.

Vandam St. **101** Spring St.

102

Dominick St.

Broome St.

1,9 M

Watts St.

Grand St. *A,C,E* M

Grand St.

Howard St.

Cleveland Pl.

Lafayette St.

Broadway

Desbrosses St.

Vestry St.

110

1,9

Canal St. **109** Lispenard St.

Walker St.

Crosby St.

Church St.

Laight St.

Hubert St.

Beach St.

Sullivan St.

White St.

Franklin St.

Thompson St.

Varick St.

Greene St.

N. Moore St. *1,9*

St. Leonard St.

112

Franklin St.

Harrison St.

Jay St.

Worth St.

Thomas St.

Duane St.

111

TRIBECA

Holland Tunnel

N

0 ___ 1800 feet

0 ___ 600 meters

MAP 6.

Listed by Site Number

Listed Alphabetically

Academy, 41. 243 W 43rd St
☎ 249-8870. Rock

A.K.A., 98. 77 W Houston
☎ 673-7325. Rock/Jazz

Algonquin, 43. 59 W44th St
☎ 840-6800. Cabaret

Apollo Theatre, 1. 253 W 125th St
☎ 749-5838. Concert Hall

Augie's Pub, 3. 2751 Broadway
☎ 864-9834. Jazz/Blues/R&B

Back Fence, 93. 155 Bleecker St
☎ 475-9221. R&R/Folk

The Bank, 108. 225 E Houston St
☎ 505-5033. Dance Club

Bar Room, 65. 432 W 14 St
☎ 366-5680. Dance/Performance Art

Beekman Bar and Books, 27.
889 First Ave ☎ 980-9314. Bar Music

Bemelman's Bar, 15. 35 E 76th St
☎ 744-1600. Bar Music

Birdland, 4. 2745 Broadway
☎ 749-2228. Jazz

Bitter End, 97. 147 Bleecker St
☎ 673-7030. Jazz/Blues/R&B

Blue Note, 88. 131 W 3rd St
☎ 475-8592. Jazz/Blues/R&B

Boston Comedy Club, 95.
82 W 3rd St ☎ 477-1000. Comedy

Bottom Line, 86. 15 W 4th St
☎ 228-6300. Folk

Bradley's, 76. 70 University Pl
☎ 228-6440. Jazz/Blues/R&B

Café Carlyle, 16. 35 E 76th St
☎ 744-1600. Hotel Lounge

Cafe 44, 38. 315 W 44th St
☎ 581-3080. Piano Bar

Cafe Pierre, 20. 2 E 61st St
☎ 940-8185. Cabaret

Cafe Wha, 91. 115 MacDougal St
☎ 254-3706. Comedy/Jazz

Cajun, 68. 129 Eighth Ave
☎ 691-6174. Jazz

Caroline's, 31. 1626 Broadway
☎ 757-4100. Comedy

CBGB & OMFUG, 104. 315 Bowery
☎ 982-4052. Punk/Rock/Dance

Chelsea Commons, 53. 242 10th Ave
☎ 929-9424. Rock/Folk

Chicago Blues, 69. 73 Eighth Ave
☎ 924-9755. Blues/Jazz

Chicago City Limits,17. 1105 First
Ave☎ 888-5233. Comedy

China Club, 8. 2130 Broadway
☎ 877-1166. Rock/Dance Club

Chippendale's, 19. 1110 First Ave
☎ 288-5788. Adult Entertainment

Club Broadway, 5. 2551 Broadway
☎ 864-7600. Reggae/Latin

Comedy Cellar, 90. 117 MacDougal
St ☎ 254-3480. Comedy

Comic Strip, 14. 1568 Second Ave
☎ 861-9386. Comedy

Continental, 85. 25 Third Ave
☎ 529-6924. Rock Club

Cooler, 66. 416 W 14th St
☎ 229-0785.

Copacabana, 24. 617 W 57th St
☎ 582-2672. Dance Club

Cornelia Street Cafe, 89.
29 Cornelia St ☎ 989-9317. Jazz

Dan Lynch's, 74. 221 Second Ave
☎ 677-0911. Blues

Dangerfield's, 18. 1118 First Ave
☎ 593-1650. Comedy

Danny's Skylight Room, 34. 346 W
46th St ☎ 265-8130. Cabaret

Don't Tell Mama, 33. 343 W 46th St
☎ 757-0788. Cabaret

Duplex, 80. 61 Christopher St
☎ 255-5438. Cabaret/Piano

The Eagle, 54. 142 Eleventh Ave
☎ 691-8451. Gay

Ear Inn, 101. 326 Spring St
☎ 226-9060. Rock/Blues

Eighty Eight's, 83. 228 W 10th St
☎ 924-0088. Cabaret

Fat Tuesday's, 64. 190 Third Ave
☎ 533-7902. Jazz/Blues/R&B

5757, 21. 57 E 57th St
☎ 758-5700. Bar Music

The Five Spot, 48. 4 W 31st St
☎ 631-0100. Jazz

Hideaway, 47. 32 W 37th St
☎ 947-8940. Ballroom/Variety

Hors D'Oeverie, 112. 1 World Trade
Center ☎ 938-1111. Jazz/Dinner

Improvisation, 52. 433 W 34th St
☎ 279-3446. Comedy

Indigo Blues, 37. 221 W 46th St
☎ 221-0033. Comedy/Brazilian

Iridium, 11. 44 W 63rd St
☎ 582-2121. Jazz

Irving Plaza, 72. 17 Irving Place
☎ 777-6800. Swing

J.J. Becketts, 60. Amsterdam at
90th St ☎ 787-9628. Bar Music

Judy's, 44. 49 W 44th St
☎ 764-8930. Piano

Kenny's Castaways, 94.
157 Bleecker St ☎ 473-9870. Rock

The Kitchen, 55. 512 W 19th St
☎ 255-5793. Jazz/Performance

Knickerbocker, 84. 33 University Pl
☎ 228-8490. Jazz

Knitting Factory, 111. 74 Leonard St
☎ 219-3055. Rock/Jazz

Laura Belle's, 42. 120 W 43rd St
☎ 819-1000. Dance/Supper Club

Le Bar Bat, 23. 311 W 57th St
☎ 307-7228. Dance Club

Limelight, 57. 660 Sixth Ave
☎ 807-7850. Dance Club

Manny's Car Wash, 13.
1558 Third Ave ☎ 369-2583. Blues

Metropolis, 63. 31 Union Square West
☎ 675-0851. Jazz

Michael's Pub, 26. 211 E 55th St
☎ 758-2272. Piano Bar/Jazz

Mondo Cane, 92. 205 Thompson St
☎ 254-5166. Blues/Jazz

Monster, 81. 80 Grove St
☎ 924-3557. Gay/Disco

Mostly Magic, 99. 55 Carmine St
☎ 924-1472. Comedy/Magic

Mercury Lounge, 107.
217 E Houston St ☎ 260-4700. Rock

Nell's, 70. 246 W 14th St
☎ 675-1567. Dance Club

New Music Cafe, 109. 285 W
Broadway ☎ 941-1019. Reggae/Rock

New York Comedy Club, 51.
241 E 24th St ☎ 696-5233. Comedy

Oak Room, 25. 59 W 44th St
☎ 840-6800. Hotel Lounge

Off Center, 10. 148 W 67th St
☎ 724-6643. Comedy

O'Lunney's, 45. 12 W 44th St
☎ 840-6688. Country/Folk

Palladium, 73. 126 E 14th St
☎ 473-7171. Dance Club

Paddy Reilly's, 49. 519 Second Ave
☎ 686-1210. Irish

Rainbow Room, 29. 30 Rockefeller
Plz ☎ 632-5000. Ballroom/Cabaret

Rainbow & Stars, 29. 30 Rockefeller
Plz ☎ 632-5000. Cabaret

Rebar, 67. Eighth Ave at 16th St
☎ 627-1680. Comedy

Red Blazer Too, 32. 349 W 46th St
☎ 262-3112. Jazz/Blues/Swing

Rock 'n Roll Cafe, 96. 149 Bleecker St
☎ 677-7630. Rock

Rodeo Bar, 50. 375 Third Ave
☎ 683-6500.
Country/Rockabilly/Blues

Roseland, 30. 239 W 52nd St
☎ 247-0200. Ballroom/Rock

Roxy, 56. 515 W 18th St
☎ 645-5156. Dance Club

Russian Tea Room, 22. 150 W 57th St
☎ 265-0947. Cabaret

Sapphire Bar, 106. 249 Eldridge St
☎ 777-5153. Funk/Soul

Sardi's, 40. 234 W 44th St
☎ 221-8444. Cabaret

Sidewalk Cafe, 103. 94 Ave A
☎ 473-7373. Jazz

Smalls, 77. 183 W 10th St
☎ 929-7565. Jazz

SOB's, 100. 204 Varick St
☎ 243-4940. Brazilian/Reggae/Jazz

Sound Factory, 59. 12 W 21st St
☎ 206-7770. Dance Club

Splash, 62. 50 W 17th St
☎ 691-0073. Gay

Stand Up NY, 7. 236 W 78th St
☎ 595-0850. Comedy

Stella Del Mare, 46. 346 Lexington
Ave ☎ 687-4425. Piano Bar

Stringfellows, 61. 35 E 21st St
☎ 254-2444. Adult Entertainment

Supper Club, 35. 240 W 47th St
☎ 921-1940. Dance/Supper Club

Sweet Basil, 82. 88 Seventh Ave S
☎ 242-1785. Jazz/Swing/Fusion

Sybarite, 102. 76 Wooster St
☎ 966-3832. Jazz

Tatou, 28. 151 E 50th St
☎ 753-1144. Dance/Supper Club

Tavern on the Green, 12. Central
Park at W 67th St ☎ 873-3200. Jazz

Terra Blues, 96. 149 Bleecker St
☎ 777-7776. Blues

Time Cafe/Fez, 105. 380 Lafayette St
☎ 533-2680. Lounge/Cabaret/Jazz

Tramps, 58. 51 W 21st St
☎ 727-7788. Blues/Country/Rock

Triad, 10. 158 W 72nd St
☎ 595-7400. Comedy

Uncle Charlie's, 78.
56 Greenwich Ave ☎ 255-8787. Gay

Vertigo, 60. 27 W 20th St
☎ 366-4181. Dance Club

Village Vanguard, 79. 178 Seventh
Ave S ☎ 255-4037. Jazz/Blues

Visiones, 87. 125 MacDougal St
☎ 673-5576. Blues/Jazz/R&B

Webster Hall, 75. 125 E 11th St
☎ 353-1600. Dance Club

West Bank Cafe, 39. 407 W 42nd St
☎ 695-6909. Comedy/Music

West End Gate, 2. 2911 Broadway
☎ 662-8830. Rock/Jazz

Wetlands, 110. 161 Hudson St
☎ 966-5244. Psychedelic Rock

Whiskey, 36. 235 W 46th St
☎ 819-0404. Bar Music

Zinno, 71. 126 W 13th St
☎ 924-5182. Blues/Jazz/R&B

MAP
61